SEEING
STARS

SARA GILLINGHAM

Φ

FOR MY GRANDMA, ETHEL GILLINGHAM, AND THE
STARRY NIGHTS WE SPENT TOGETHER ON KEATS ISLAND
AND
FOR ELLIS GARTNER, UP WITH THE STARS

Dear Reader,

As you will learn in this book, a constellation is a group of bright stars that forms
a picture when imaginary lines are drawn between the stars to connect them. These
pictures in the sky have inspired people to tell stories about constellations for
thousands of years.

In this book you will learn about the 88 official constellations that are defined
by the International Astronomical Union (IAU). However, there is no "official" way
of connecting the stars of a constellation, and no "correct" picture that goes with it.
So I decided to follow the connected-line constellation shapes that are most common
and, wherever possible, my illustrations of the characters, animals, and objects
have been designed to line up with the constellation shapes so that they are easy
to remember and recognize when you see them in the sky.

Just as there are many visual interpretations of constellations, there are countless
stories that relate to them. My aim was to choose the most well-known or most
interesting myths and legends associated with each constellation, but there are many
more tales out there for those who wish to know!

My hope is that these images and stories will introduce you to the stars and inspire
you, just as they have inspired storytellers and artists over so many thousands of years.

When looking up at the stars, I like to think of all the other people who have
looked up at the same sky over time, and imagine a zillion tiny lines connecting
us all, just like the lines that connect our stars to create constellations.

— S.G.

ACKNOWLEDGMENTS

Just like a constellation, this book could
not exist without a group of bright stars:

Senior Editor Maya Gartner, for
exceptional guidance and dedication
Art Director Meagan Bennett, for
inspired and tireless art direction
and design
Astronomer Paul Murdin, for vital
expertise and consultation
Publisher Cecily Kaiser, for visionary
support
Designer Michelle Clement, for crucial
assistance with maps
Production experts Rebecca Price and
Elaine Ward, for making this book shine

Special thanks to the following consultants
for their research/vetting of this book:
Janine Alyson Young; Craig Campbell,
Associate Professor, Anthropology; J.R.C.
Cousland, Associate Professor of Classical,
Near Eastern and Religious Studies; Seemi
Ghazi, Lecturer in Classical Arabic; Ibrahim
Atef Saker; Michael Reid, Associate
Professor, Astronomy.

CONTENTS

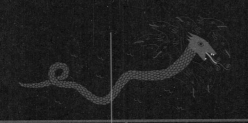

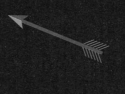

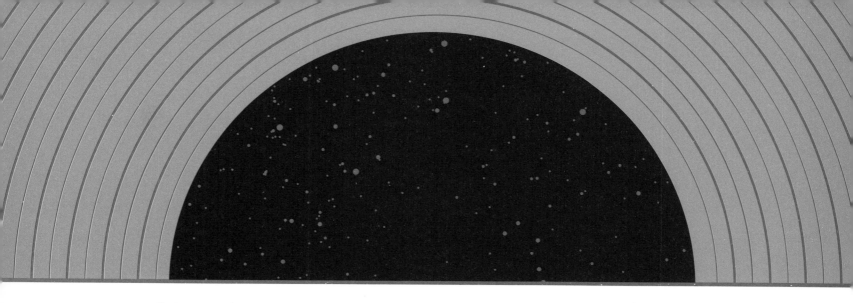

SEEING PICTURES IN THE SKY

STARS AND THEIR STORIES

Imagine that it is nighttime and you are in the countryside, far away from street lamps and car headlights. There are no lit-up buildings or skyscrapers near you. It's so dark that it's hard to see *anything* around you. You look up and see that the sky is bright with the glow of stars. Some stars are brighter than others, or clustered together in interesting shapes and patterns. As you continue to watch the stars, some of these patterns start to look like familiar things. One might look like a hook and another like a giant spoon. These shapes and images might remind you of a story you've heard, or inspire you to make up your own.

In ancient times, people around the world looked up at the stars, night after night. They began to see pictures in the sky. In one part of the sky, some people saw an arrangement of bright stars that looked like a fish, and in another, they saw a set of stars that resembled a lumbering bear. These stargazers saw characters and objects in the stars that reminded them of the myths and stories they knew. Many different cultures created their own stories as well. These stories were shared between families, friends, and villages, and passed down from one generation to the next. Each time they were passed on, different details and layers were added. Sometimes stories were adapted or even changed, until eventually, somebody decided to write down the stories and pictures. Today, we know these pictures in the sky as CONSTELLATIONS!

✳   ✳   ✳

WHAT ARE CONSTELLATIONS?

A constellation is a group of bright stars that forms a picture when imaginary lines are drawn between the stars. It's like playing a game of "connect the dots" in the sky!

Although many cultures have identified constellations, it was the ancient Greek and later European cultures that passed down the 88 official constellations that are now used around the world by scientists who study the stars. These scientists are called astronomers, and constellations help them find their way around the sky. Constellations also tell stories of creatures, characters, and objects that people have shared over thousands of years. For example, there are constellations that tell the story of a ship that sailed through dangerous waters carrying

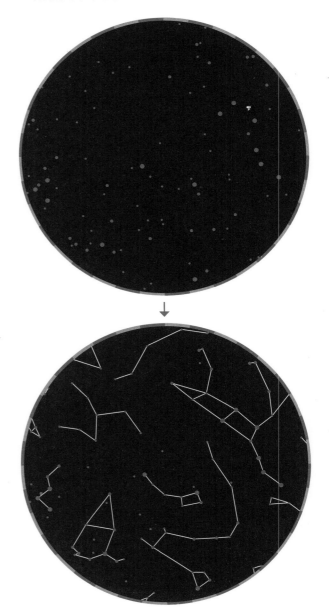

a host of heroes on a quest for a mythical treasure that no one believed could be found. Another constellation portrays a dragon that guards a tree with apples that can make you live forever. Constellations aren't just about stars — they are about stories, too!

✳ ✳ ✳

WHO INVENTED THE 88 CONSTELLATIONS?

Storytellers and **navigators** have known and used the 88 constellations for many thousands of years, but about 2,300 years ago, they were written down by a Greek astronomer called Eudoxus and then copied by a Greek poet called Aratus. A few hundred years later, a man called Ptolemy (pronounced Tol-o-mee) made a list and drawings of all the stars in the constellations in a famous book called *Almagest*. Ptolemy's list is the basis of the official system of constellations that scientists use today.

Almost 1,000 years later, and more than 1,000 miles away, a Persian astronomer named al-Sufi translated Ptolemy's book into Arabic and added his own observations of the stars. Al-Sufi's book included illustrations of the constellations and incorporated Arabic star names. His methods and observations were so advanced for the time, they were adopted all over the world. Several centuries after the first handwritten book copies made their way across Europe, al-Sufi's book was translated into Latin, which had become the established language for scientists to share their discoveries. This is why you will see Greek, Arabic, and Latin words in the constellation and star names!

Ptolemy and al-Sufi could not travel far enough to see all the stars in the southern **hemisphere**, but hundreds of years later, when Italian, French, Dutch, and Polish explorers set off to explore the southern seas, they saw many new stars for the first time and new constellations were mapped in the sky.

When telescopes were invented 500 years ago, astronomers were able to see more in the sky than ever before. Multitudes of stars were "discovered" — and they needed names! Astronomers named things in different ways, and the constellations got into a bit of a muddle. So, in 1922, a group of astronomers from around the world (known as the International Astronomical Union, or the **IAU**), felt it was time to make an official map of the sky for *all* astronomers around the globe. They decided on 88 official constellations and divided the sky into 88 sections — similar to how the borders of countries are marked on world maps. Each section was named after the constellation inside it.

Today, astronomers still use the name of a constellation to refer to its section in the sky.

✳   ✳   ✳

USING THIS BOOK

This book will show you how to recognize and spot the 88 official constellations in the sky, and tell you the stories behind them all! For each constellation, you'll find an image of its connect-the-dot shape, a "how-to-find-it" map that shows you where it sits in relation

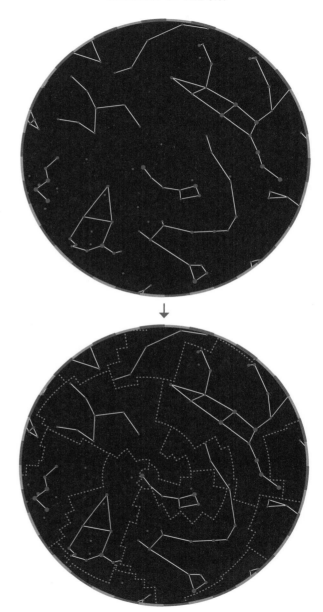

to other constellations in the sky, and an illustration of the character, object, or creature for which the constellation is named. You may notice that some illustrations are orientated differently to the maps. This is so you can enjoy them right-side up! There is also information about when the constellation is best seen and any important stars or **asterisms** that it contains.

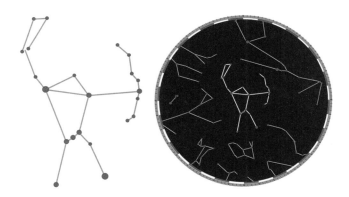

CONSTELLATION SHAPE AND HOW-TO-FIND-IT MAP FOR ORION

This book is organized into two sections so that you know which constellations are ancient (from thousands of years ago) and which ones are "modern" (created during the Age of Exploration in the 1500s to 1700s). It also has useful resources at the back to help you with your stargazing, and a glossary describing the special words highlighted in

bold throughout the book. The more you know about the shapes of the constellations and the stories behind them, the more exciting it will be when you spot them in the sky!

* * *

WHAT'S AN ASTERISM?

An asterism is a small pattern or group of stars — often, but not always, within or part of a constellation — that is not officially recognized by the **IAU**. Some people think that the Big Dipper is a constellation, but it is actually an asterism, and part of the Ursa Major constellation. Not all cultures see the same asterisms, so their names and shapes can vary.

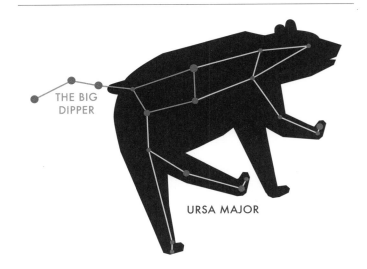

THE BIG DIPPER

URSA MAJOR

LOOK OUT FOR THE BRIGHTEST STARS

Stars in the night sky don't always look alike. Some are bright and some are faint. Astronomers use a measurement called "magnitude" to represent a star's brightness. This is why the stars in this book have different sizes. The large connect-the-dot diagrams have three different star sizes to illustrate their levels of brightness (although astronomers use more, as you will see in the

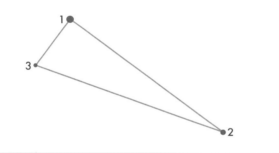

sky maps). The largest circles represent the brightest stars, the medium ones represent the fairly bright stars, and the smallest illustrate faint stars. When looking for a constellation, the easiest way to find it is to look for its brightest star first. In the full-page character, creature, and object illustrations, the brightest star has a special glow so that you know which one to look out for.

Did you know that the Sun is also a star? It's the brightest star in our sky! It's so bright that we can't see all the other stars in the sky until the Sun sets. The brightest stars in our night sky are called **first magnitude stars**. There are 21 of them, not including the Sun, and they are marked in the illustrations like this:

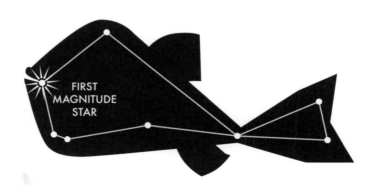

You may notice that some stars have two names, like "Sadalsuud (Beta Aquarii)." This is because this star has a well-known historical name — Sadalsuud — as well as a "designation" or scientific name in Latin — Beta Aquarii. In this book, stars without historical names are just referred to by their Latin designations.

✳   ✳   ✳

WHICH CONSTELLATIONS CAN I SEE?

Before you begin stargazing, it is important to know that the constellations you will be able to see depend on where you live — especially in which **hemisphere** — and the time of year. The **equator** is an imaginary line that divides our planet into two even sections: what's above the equator is called the northern hemisphere, and what's below is called the southern hemisphere. The United States, Europe, China, and Russia are located in the northern hemisphere. Places in the southern hemisphere include Australia, New Zealand, South America, the lower parts of Africa, and the many island nations that surround it. You can't see a constellation in the southern sky if you live too far north — or vice versa — unless you travel there! However, the

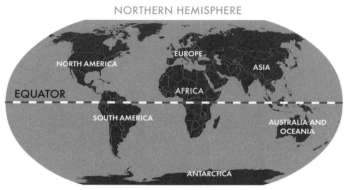

equatorial constellations, which circle the sky above the middle of Earth, can be seen from most places in the world.

Because of the way Earth spins on its axis and **orbits** the Sun, some constellations can be seen all year round. These constellations are called **circumpolar** (which roughly means "circling the poles") because they appear to move around at the top of the sky. In the northern hemisphere, some of the circumpolar constellations are Camelopardalis, Cassiopeia, Cepheus, Draco, Ursa Major, and Ursa Minor. In the southern hemisphere, some of them are Carina, Centaurus, and Crux. Other constellations are only visible during certain seasons due to Earth's tilt toward or away from the Sun throughout the year. For instance, in the northern hemisphere, Orion can only be seen during the winter.

The viewing dates in the how-to-find-it sections are for a 9pm viewing time, though the constellation may be visible for shorter or longer periods of time based on your location. There is also a section at the back of the book with sky maps to show you the orientation of constellations at different times of the year.

✳   ✳   ✳

STARGAZING

The best kind of night for viewing stars is when the sky is clear. A full moon can wash out the light from the stars, so it's best to look for stars when the Moon is new or not visible, or at least not full.

The best place from which to view stars and constellations is outside of cities, because the lights from tall buildings and cars make the stars hard to see. If you are in the city, try to find a place that doesn't have a lot of light nearby. Don't try to stargaze from underneath a street lamp, for example! And let your eyes adjust to the dark for about 15

minutes — you'll be able to see more stars that way. A balcony, a rooftop, or the middle of a large park can be good places from which to view stars in a city. Many cities also have observatories, which are places dedicated to viewing the stars.

Stars are not only beautiful to look at, they have also been important to humankind for many reasons since ancient times. Before there were maps or GPS, stars helped sailors and travelers navigate, or find their way around the world. Before there were calendars, stars helped farmers predict the seasons so they could successfully plant their crops. And before movies and the Internet, and even before printed books, the patterns and shapes the stars made were a way to retell the stories and legends of different cultures and make up new ones.

Just because the stories of the constellations are written down, it doesn't mean that they are finished! The stories can still develop and change, as they have over thousands of years. You, too, can be a part of those stories, discovering the mystery and history of the stars. All you have to do is look up!

THE ANCIENT CONSTELLATIONS

While the images in the constellations were created by the earliest cultures thousands of years ago, and astronomers had begun to record them, it was a Greek mathematician-geographer-astronomer, Claudius Ptolemy, who first made a list of these stars and their constellations. *Almagest*, his book documenting the stars, was written in the year 150 — almost 2,000 years ago! Although Ptolemy was born in Egypt and was a citizen of Rome, he was Greek and that's why the stories he collected included many important characters and stories from Greek mythology. As he put together *Almagest*, Ptolemy also studied texts from Babylon, where an ancient culture thrived over 3,000 years ago, and Sumeria, where an important civilization flourished almost 7,000 years ago. Both of these empires were located in what we know today as Iraq and Kuwait and they had a great interest in studying the stars.

Then, just over 1,000 years ago, the astronomer al-Sufi, who lived in what is now modern-day Iran, researched and added to Ptolemy's work. His own book — the title translates to *The Book of Fixed Stars* — included illustrations of the constellations and the Arabic star names. One challenge was that Ptolemy didn't name many stars in his book, but instead, he described them, for example, as "There are three bright stars in a straight line forming the arm." Al-Sufi gave these stars names, and also made notes about their magnitude, which is a system for recording a star's brightness in relation to others. The lower the number assigned to it, the brighter the star. His methods and observations were adopted all over the world.

Ptolemy and al-Sufi recorded 48 constellations, which are some of the oldest and best known in the sky today. We've called them the "ancient constellations," and you will get to know them in the following two sections called "The Zodiac" and "Myths and Legends."

THE
ZODIAC

The zodiac is a belt of 13 constellations that are lined up in a circle around Earth called the **ecliptic**, a set path in the sky along which the Sun appears to travel. Every year, Earth makes one turn around the Sun, showing us a different view of the zodiac constellations as it turns. Which one of the constellations we can see in the sky gives us a hint about which month it is. This is how the zodiac constellations helped ancient cultures create the first calendars! These constellations are mostly animals, and the word "zodiac" means "little circle of animals." To the ancient Greeks, zodiac constellations often told stories that helped them make what they thought were good choices in life.

You might have heard the word "zodiac" before when people talked about star signs, astrological signs, or horoscopes. Only twelve of the constellations in the zodiac are astrological signs: Ophiuchus is not included. These things are part of **astrology**, which is the non-scientific study of the stars and planets with the belief that the stars are a powerful force that affects our life on Earth. Unlike **astronomy**, astrology is not a science, but it was inspired by the zodiac constellations!

AQUARIUS

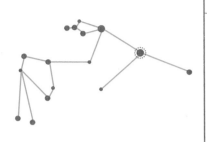

LOCATION: EQUATORIAL

Aquarius is one of the largest and oldest constellations in the sky. Its stars make up the shape of a person holding something.

HOW TO FIND IT

Aquarius is best seen between late Sept. and Dec. from nearly everywhere on Earth where people live.

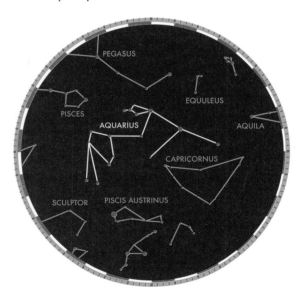

STORIES AND MYTHS

Aquarius means "water-" or "cup-carrier" in Latin and, although there are many ancient stories associated with this arrangement of stars, the tale of Ganymede — a handsome Greek prince — is one of the most well-known. In ancient Greek times, Ganymede was considered the most beautiful man alive. Word of his beauty traveled, and one day, in the middle of a quiet life tending sheep, Ganymede was snatched by an eagle and taken to **Zeus**, the ruler of the **gods of Mount Olympus**. There he was handed a water jar and put to work as the official cup-bearer to the gods.

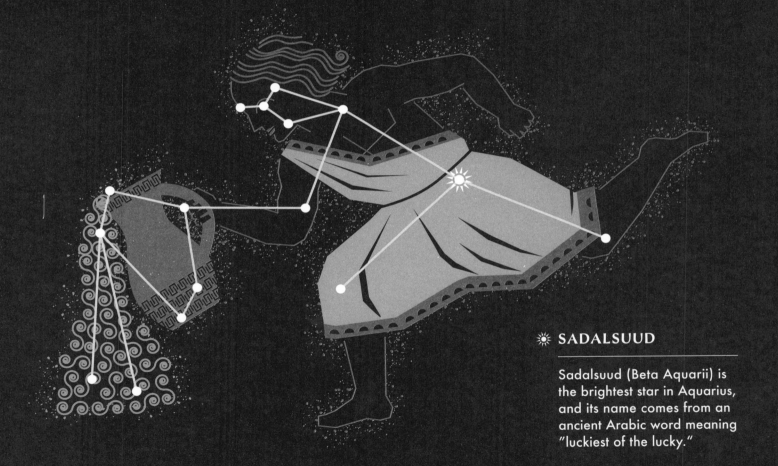

☀ **SADALSUUD**

Sadalsuud (Beta Aquarii) is the brightest star in Aquarius, and its name comes from an ancient Arabic word meaning "luckiest of the lucky."

ARIES

Aries is a medium-sized constellation whose stars join to form a slightly curved line.

HOW TO FIND IT

Aries is best seen between late Sept. and late Dec. from nearly everywhere on Earth where people live.

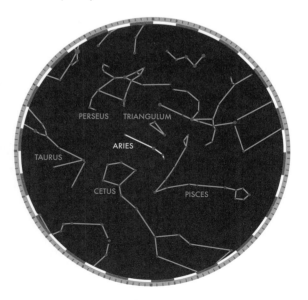

STORIES AND MYTHS

Aries is Latin for "ram" or "male sheep." In Greek mythology, there was a mythical ram with a golden coat of wool, or "fleece." When a young prince named Phrixus was about to be sacrificed to the gods, his mother sent this special golden ram to carry him away to safety. Phrixus was so grateful to be saved that he sacrificed the ram to **Zeus** — and the ram's Golden Fleece was treasured and guarded so that nobody could take it. Many years later, Jason, a hero who had his kingship stolen from him by his uncle, sailed his ship, the *Argo*, on an epic journey to find and bring back the Golden Fleece to prove himself worthy of the throne. With his crew of heroes, the Argonauts, Jason overcame many challenges to recover the fleece and become the rightful king.

THE RAM

☀ **HAMAL**

Hamal (Alpha Arietis) is the brightest star in Aries and comes from an Arabic word for the 'child of a sheep'.

CANCER

LOCATION: NORTHERN HEMISPHERE

Cancer is a medium-sized constellation, and its stars make up a shape that looks like the letter Y, which is sometimes sideways or upside down, depending on when you look at it.

HOW TO FIND IT

Cancer is best seen between late March and June from nearly everywhere on Earth where people live.

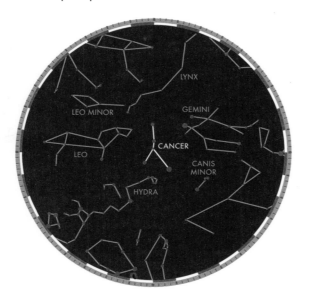

STORIES AND MYTHS

The stars in Cancer are the faintest in the zodiac, and the story of the constellation in Greek mythology is just as slight. It appears quickly in the tale of one of the greatest heroes, Hercules (known as Heracles in Greek, but better known for his Roman name). Hercules, the son of **Zeus**, had to perform 12 tasks, or "labors," in order to pay for a terrible crime he committed. His second task was to destroy a water monster called the Hydra, which was a favorite beast of Hera, Zeus's wife. When it seemed that Hercules was winning, Hera sent a giant crab to cause trouble, but Hercules, who was known for his incredible strength, easily crushed the crab with his foot. Hera put the crab in the sky as a reward for its service.

THE CRAB

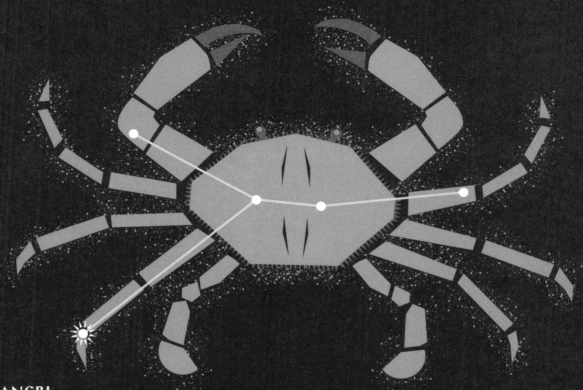

☀ BETA CANCRI

Beta Cancri is the brightest
star in Cancer, and is
sometimes called Al Tarf —
from an Arabic phrase that
means "the end."

CAPRICORNUS

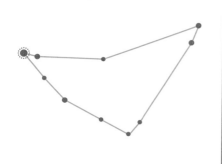

LOCATION: SOUTHERN HEMISPHERE

Capricornus is a medium-sized constellation whose stars make an irregular triangle shape.

HOW TO FIND IT

Capricornus is best seen between late June and Sept. everywhere except the northern-most parts of the northern **hemisphere**.

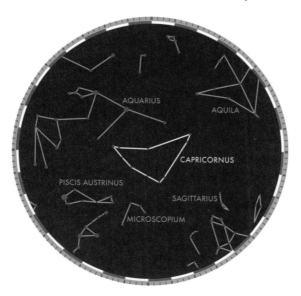

STORIES AND MYTHS

Capricornus, also known as Capricorn, is called a sea goat, or goat fish, with the front legs and head of a goat, and the body of a fish. In Greek myths, the sea goat symbolizes Pan, the god of shepherds, hunters, and the wild. Pan was part goat, part man, which the Greeks called a **satyr** or a faun. The word "panic" comes from Pan, as he had the power to terrify people with his loud snorting noises. He is also known for inventing the pan pipes, a musical instrument made out of reeds. When one of the deadliest monsters in Greek mythology, Typhon, tried to overthrow the gods, Pan warned them, and then gave himself the tail of a fish and escaped into a river. He was transformed into the constellation Capricornus while in the form of the sea goat.

THE SEA GOAT

☀ DELTA CAPRICORNI

Delta Capricorni is the brightest star in Capricornus and is sometimes called Deneb Algedi, from an Arabic phrase for "tail of the goat."

GEMINI

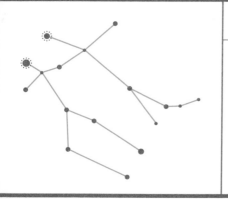

Gemini is a medium-sized constellation with a lot of stars that can be seen without a telescope. Its stars form a shape that looks like two figures holding hands!

HOW TO FIND IT

Gemini is best seen between late Dec. and March from nearly everywhere on Earth where people live.

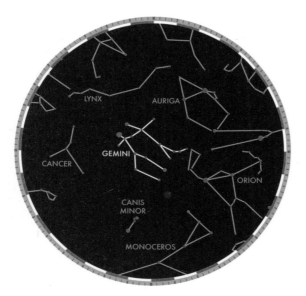

STORIES AND MYTHS

The twins pictured here in Gemini are Castor and Pollux (Polydeuces in Greek), sons of Leda, queen of Sparta, from Greek mythology. Pollux's father was a god, so he was **immortal**, but Castor was **mortal**, because his father was a man. Castor was a strong warrior and horse rider, and Pollux was a talented boxer. The twins were best friends and heroes. They sailed alongside Jason and his crew of Argonauts aboard the famous ship, *Argo*, on their quest for the Golden Fleece. Castor and Pollux had special nautical powers given to them by Poseidon, the god of the sea, with which they kept the *Argo* safe through many dangers. When Castor died, **Zeus** agreed to make him immortal so that he and Pollux would never be apart, and he placed them together in the sky.

THE TWINS

POLLUX

Pollux (Beta Geminorum)
is a first magnitude star,
the 17th brightest in the sky,
and the brightest in Gemini.

CASTOR

Castor (Alpha Geminorum)
is the second brightest star
in Gemini.

LEO

LOCATION: EQUATORIAL

Leo is one of the biggest constellations, whose connected stars look a lot like a lion!

HOW TO FIND IT

Leo is best seen between late March and June from nearly everywhere on Earth where people live.

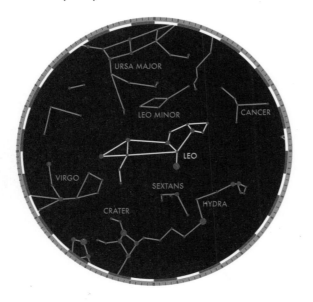

STORIES AND MYTHS

Many ancient cultures saw a lion in these stars, but for the Greeks, this was the lion of Nemea, an enormous beast that could not be killed by any weapon. Hercules was sent to battle the lion for his first task. But his arrows and club would simply bounce off the lion's skin! Hercules finally defeated the lion by choking it with his bare hands. Then he made a cloak out of the lion's skin using the lion's own claws. This cloak protected him during his other dangerous tasks.

THE LION

REGULUS

Regulus (Alpha Leonis) is Latin for "little king." It is a first magnitude star, the 21st brightest star in the sky, and the brightest star in Leo.

LIBRA

Libra is one of the larger constellations, whose stars make a triangular shape, with two straight lines coming down from either side. It looks a lot like an old-fashioned two-sided balancing scale.

HOW TO FIND IT

Libra is best seen between late June and Sept. from nearly everywhere on Earth where people live.

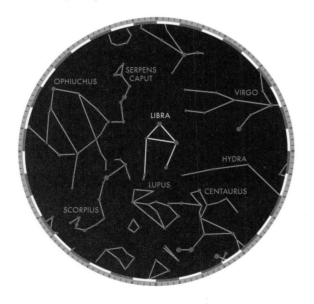

STORIES AND MYTHS

Libra means "scales" in Latin and sits near the feet of the constellation Virgo. Some stories say that these scales belong to her. Unlike our scales today, which have one surface or pan that things are placed on for weighing, ancient scales used two pans, and compared the weight of one side to the other. The ancient Romans considered Libra one of their favorite constellations, because, for them, the idea of balancing two sides of a scale represented fairness, justice, and harmony.

THE SCALES

Zubeneschamali (Beta Librae) is the brightest star in Libra. Its name comes from the "northern claw" in Arabic, because Libra's scales used to be viewed as the claws of the constellation Scorpius.

OPHIUCHUS

LOCATION: EQUATORIAL

Ophiuchus is a large constellation whose stars make up a crooked-house shape. It is interlinked with the constellation Serpens. Although Ophiuchus sits within the zodiac constellations, it is not considered an official astrological sign of the zodiac.

HOW TO FIND IT

Ophiuchus is best seen between late June and Sept. from nearly everywhere on Earth where people live.

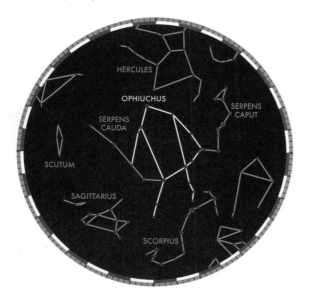

STORIES AND MYTHS

Ophiuchus — which comes from a Greek word for "serpent-bearer" — is represented by Asclepius, the god of medicine. He is pictured here holding the snake in the constellation Serpens, because, while most people look at snakes and see danger, Asclepius came to see them as healers. One day, after Asclepius killed a snake, another snake slithered over to place an herb on the dead snake's body and it came back to life. Asclepius tried the snake's trick and placed the same herb on the body of a young prince who had just died, and he, too, came back to life!

THE SERPENT HOLDER

☀ RASALHAGUE

Rasalhague (Alpha Ophiuchi)
comes from Arabic for
the "head of the serpent
collector" and is the brightest
star in Ophiuchus.

PISCES

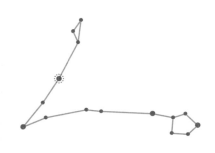

Pisces is a large but faint constellation, whose stars form the shape of a **polygon** and a triangle attached by a V-shaped line.

HOW TO FIND IT

Pisces is best seen between late Sept. and Dec. from nearly everywhere on Earth where people live.

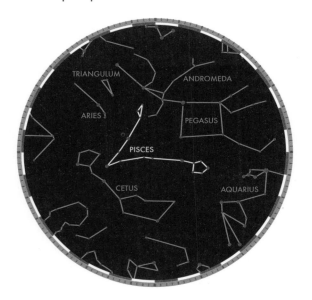

STORIES AND MYTHS

In Greek mythology, after the epic War of the **Titans**, where the **gods of Mount Olympus** overthrew the Titans as rulers of Earth, **Gaia**, the mother of the Titans and the earth goddess, became very angry. She sent a terrifying, serpent-like monster called Typhon to punish the gods of Mount Olympus. In their effort to escape, Aphrodite, the goddess of love, and her son Eros, the god of love, turned themselves into *pisces* — Latin for "fishes" — so they could slip into the Euphrates river and escape the vicious monster. They tied their tails together with a cord so that they wouldn't lose each other in the water.

THE FISHES

☀ ETA PISCIUM

Eta Piscium is the brightest star in Pisces, and was originally called Kullat Nūnu, from an ancient Babylonian phrase for the "cord of the fish."

SAGITTARIUS

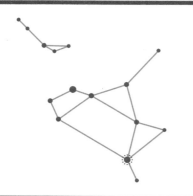

LOCATION: SOUTHERN HEMISPHERE

Sagittarius is one of the biggest constellations in the sky and its eight brightest stars form a complex shape that includes a very well-known **asterism** called the Teapot.

HOW TO FIND IT

Sagittarius is best seen between late June and Sept. from anywhere except the top third of the northern **hemisphere**.

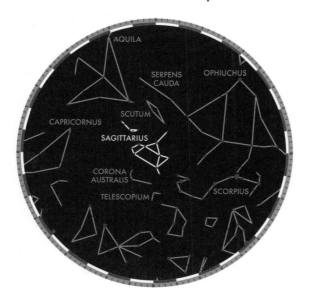

STORIES AND MYTHS

The **centaur** (half-human, half-horse) pictured in Sagittarius — Latin for "archer" — was adopted by the Greeks from earlier myths that existed in Mesopotamian, Sumerian, and Babylonian cultures, which called it Pabilsag. Pabilsag, a human, was a great hunter, but when he was placed in the sky, he was given the legs of a horse to acknowledge his skill as a rider. In some Greek myths, Sagittarius is said to represent the god Crotus, known as the inventor of archery. Like Pabilsag, Crotus was an excellent hunter and horse rider. Sagittarius's arrow points directly at the constellation Scorpius. It is said that Sagittarius was specifically placed near Scorpius to warn it not to leave its place in the sky and cause trouble!

THE ARCHER

☀ KAUS AUSTRALIS

Kaus Australis (Epsilon Sagittarii) comes from Latin for "southern part of the bow" and is the brightest star in Sagittarius.

ASTERISM

Teapot

SCORPIUS

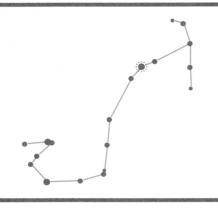

Scorpius is a large constellation with many bright stars. Its stars form the shape of a scorpion: an *S*-like curve with two clawlike lines on one side.

HOW TO FIND IT

Scorpius is best seen between late June and Sept. from the southern **hemisphere**, and the bottom half of the northern hemisphere.

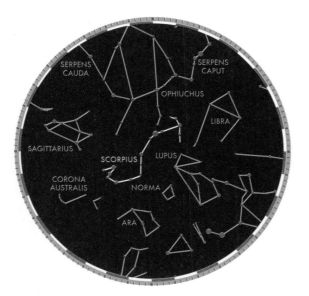

STORIES AND MYTHS

With its notable curving shape, this constellation was pictured as a scorpion by Babylonians long before the ancient Greeks borrowed it for their famous story. In the Greek myth, the talented hunter Orion bragged that he could hunt every animal on Earth if he wanted to. Hearing this, the earth goddess **Gaia** sent a scorpion to kill Orion as punishment for his boasting. **Zeus** made the scorpion into a constellation as a reminder for people to keep their pride in check. It is said that Orion is best seen during the winter because he avoids Scorpius, who climbs high in the sky during the summer.

THE SCORPION

 **ANTARES**

Antares (Alpha Scorpii) is a striking red color, the most noticeably colored star in the sky, and that is the origin of its name Antares, which comes from a Greek word for "like Mars." It is a first magnitude star, the 16th brightest star in the sky, and the brightest star in Scorpius.

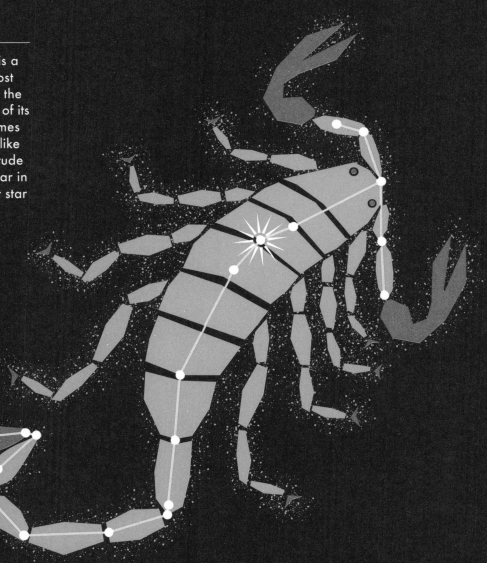

TAURUS

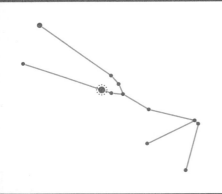

Taurus is a large and easy-to-find constellation whose stars make a line with a big V shape at the top, and a smaller one at the bottom. Taurus contains two well-known asterisms: the Hyades and the Pleiades.

HOW TO FIND IT

Taurus is best seen between late Dec. and March from nearly everywhere on Earth where people live.

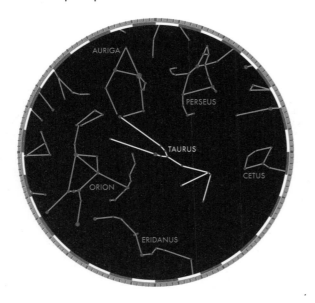

STORIES AND MYTHS

Taurus — Latin for "bull" — is one of the oldest constellations in the sky. Some archaeologists believe that a 15,000-year-old cave painting shows Taurus and the Pleiades! In Greek myths, Taurus is associated with **Zeus**, who often disguised himself as a bull. In one story, in his bull disguise, Zeus swam to the island of Crete, which may explain why we only see the top half of Taurus's body — the bottom half was hidden in the water. The cluster of stars near the bull's back is called the Pleiades, also known as the Seven Sisters, though only six stars are visible to the naked eye. The Hyades were half-sisters of the Pleiades. It is said that they died of grief when their brother, Hyas, was killed, and this is why they were placed in the sky.

THE BULL

Pleiades

Hyades

ALDEBARAN

Aldebaran (Alpha Tauri) comes from an Arabic word for the "follower," possibly because it follows the Pleiades asterism through the sky. It is a first magnitude star, the 14th brightest in the sky, and the brightest star in Taurus.

VIRGO

LOCATION: EQUATORIAL

Virgo is the second largest constellation in the sky. Its stars are easy to find: they form the shape of a person with a diamond-shaped head.

HOW TO FIND IT

Virgo is best seen between late March and June from nearly everywhere on Earth where people live.

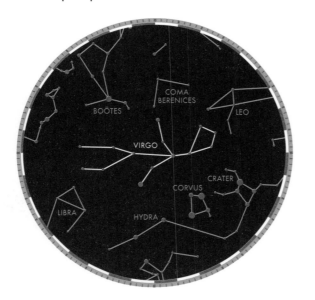

STORIES AND MYTHS

Virgo is the Latin word for an innocent maiden. In some ancient Greek stories, this constellation was thought to be Dike, a winged goddess. Dike lived at a time when the world was peaceful, happy, and beautiful. This all changed when **Zeus** overthrew his father, **Cronus**. Humans began to treat one another badly and peace was gone. Dike tried to warn the humans that it would only get worse. When they did not listen, and the world descended into a dark time of war and violence, Dike left Earth forever. She is pictured above the scales of Libra (the scales of justice) and symbolizes innocence, fertility, and high moral standards.

THE VIRGIN

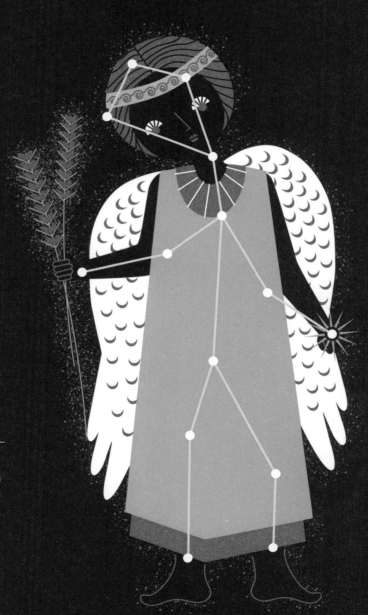

SPICA

Spica (Alpha Virginis) is a first magnitude star, the 15th brightest star in the sky, and the brightest star in Virgo.

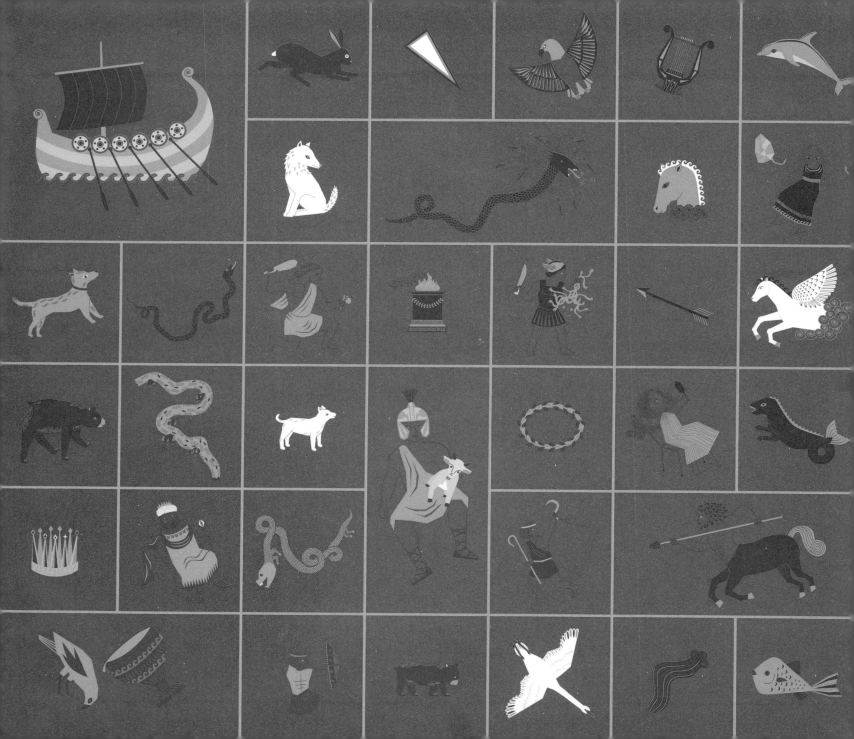

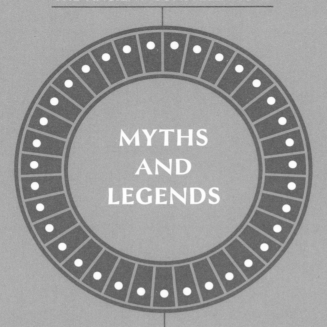

MYTHS AND LEGENDS

In addition to the zodiac constellations, there were many others created and mapped in ancient times. These include well-known stories, characters, animals, and sacred objects from Greek mythology, as well as gods and heroes who you've probably heard of before, such as the mighty Hercules, one of the most famous Greek heroes of all time.

Imagine gazing up into the sky and seeing a constellation that tells the story of a hero who battles a vicious sea monster in order to help an unfortunate princess, and then rides away on a mythical winged horse. Well, in Greek mythology, the sea monster is called Cetus, the princess is Andromeda, and the mythical winged horse is Pegasus — and they are all constellations! The hero is none other than the legendary slayer of monsters, Perseus, who is also a constellation. And guess what? These four constellations are located near one another in the sky!

After you read the stories, look at the sky maps carefully, and you'll find that many of the constellations with connected stories sit near each other in the sky.

ANDROMEDA

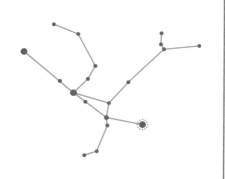

Andromeda is a large constellation in a complicated shape with many bright stars. Andromeda's brightest star is part of an **asterism** called the Great Square of Pegasus.

HOW TO FIND IT

Andromeda is best seen between late Sept. and Dec. from anywhere except the bottom half of the southern **hemisphere**.

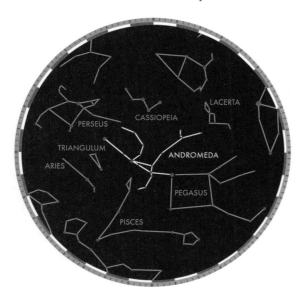

STORIES AND MYTHS

Andromeda was a princess known for her kindness and beauty. One day her proud mother, Queen Cassiopeia, boasted that her daughter was more beautiful than the **Nereids**, the famously beautiful sea nymphs. This made the Nereids so angry and jealous that they asked Poseidon, god of the sea, to punish the family. A vicious sea monster, Cetus, was sent by Poseidon to terrorize the nearby coast. Andromeda's father, King Cepheus, was told that the only way to stop Cetus was to offer the terrible creature his wonderful, innocent daughter. Andromeda was chained to a rock as a sacrifice, but just before the sea monster gobbled her up, a kind hero, Perseus, killed the monster and unchained Andromeda. Then the two rode away on the winged horse, Pegasus.

THE CHAINED LADY

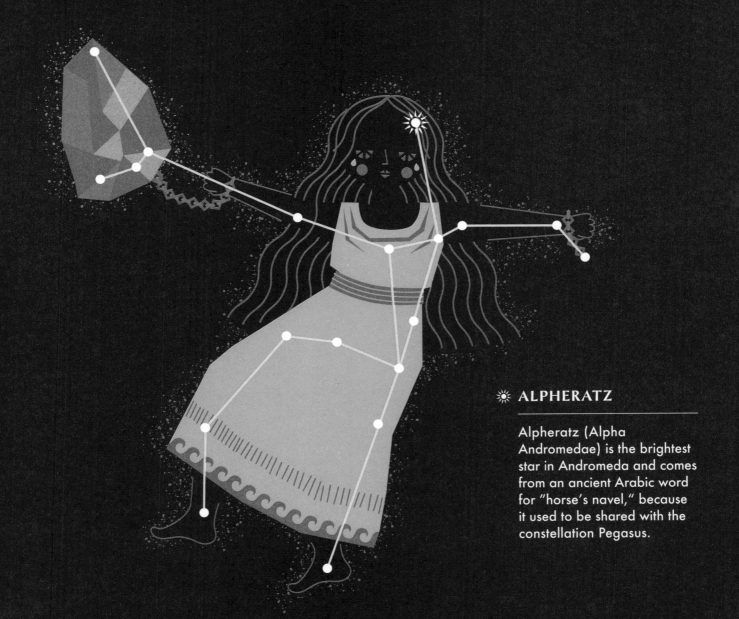

☀ ALPHERATZ

Alpheratz (Alpha Andromedae) is the brightest star in Andromeda and comes from an ancient Arabic word for "horse's navel," because it used to be shared with the constellation Pegasus.

AQUILA

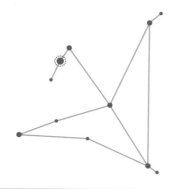

LOCATION: EQUATORIAL

Aquila is one of the larger constellations, and its stars make up a shape that looks a lot like a bird!

HOW TO FIND IT

Aquila is best seen between late June and Sept. from nearly everywhere on Earth where people live.

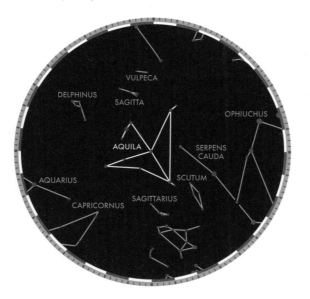

STORIES AND MYTHS

Aquila, which means "eagle" in Latin, was **Zeus's** personal messenger in the ancient Greek myths. He had the dangerous-sounding job of carrying and retrieving the many thunderbolts that Zeus threw at his enemies. The constellation Aquila sits very near to Aquarius, and is connected to the story of Aquarius because Aquila is thought to have been the eagle that was sent by Zeus to snatch the Greek prince Ganymede from his quiet field to become the water carrier to the gods. In other stories, however, Zeus changes himself into an eagle, or turns others into eagles, in order to fulfill his wishes.

THE EAGLE

ALTAIR

Altair (Alpha Aquilae) is a
first magnitude star, the 12th
brightest in the sky, and the
brightest star in Aquila. This
star was associated with
an eagle long before the
ancient Greeks and its name
comes from an Arabic word
for "flying eagle."

ARA

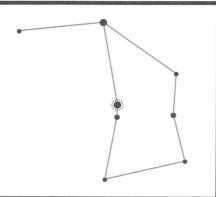

LOCATION: SOUTHERN HEMISPHERE

Ara is a small constellation. Its stars make an irregular **polygon** shape that was often associated with an altar: a large table or stone blocks on which people used to place offerings to the gods.

HOW TO FIND IT

Ara is best seen between late June and late Sept. from the southern **hemisphere**, and in southern parts of the northern hemisphere.

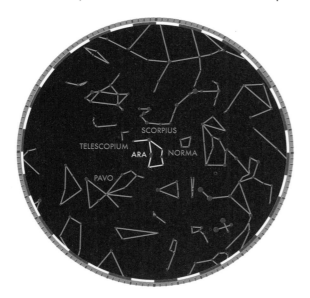

STORIES AND MYTHS

In ancient times, people placed gifts of meat, food, or other precious items on altars and burned them as sacrifices in order to please the gods. The ancient Greeks made these offerings in hope that the gods would help them with their troubles. Ara is thought to be a special altar that the gods themselves used. One of the most important stories of ancient Greece was how **Zeus** overthrew the **Titans**, who ruled the universe before him. Before the War of the Titans, Zeus and his allies made a vow in front of an altar to overthrow the Titans together; Ara most likely represents this altar, and the **Milky Way** (which is located near Ara) is said to represent the smoke from the altar's fire.

THE ALTAR

☀ BETA ARAE

Beta Arae is the brightest star in Ara. It is sometimes called Vasat-ül-cemre, which comes from Turkish for "middle of fire."

ARGO NAVIS: CARINA, PUPPIS, VELA

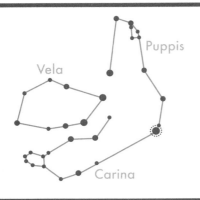

Carina, Puppis, and Vela are three constellations that used to be part of a large constellation that made the shape of a sailing ship called the *Argo Navis*, which means "the ship Argo" in Latin. *Carina* is Latin for "the keel (bottom) of a ship"; *puppis,* "the stern (back) of a ship"; and *vela,* "the sail."

HOW TO FIND IT

They are best seen from late Dec. to March from the southern **hemisphere** and the bottom half of the northern hemisphere.

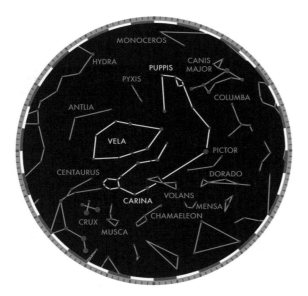

STORIES AND MYTHS

The *Argo* was said to be the first ship ever to be built and its captain was Jason, son of the king of Iolcus. Jason was next in line to be king when his uncle Pelias stole the throne for himself. Pelias promised Jason that he could win back his right to be king if he could find and bring back the Golden Fleece, the coat of the mystical ram with golden wool. Jason assembled a crew of Greek heroes called the Argonauts to sail the Black Sea in search of the fleece. The Greek word for sailor is *nautes,* which is why the crew was called the Argonauts. After a very long and dangerous voyage on the *Argo,* the heroes returned with the fleece and Jason became king. Athena, the goddess of wisdom and strategy, placed the *Argo* among the constellations to commemorate the ship.

THE KEEL, THE STERN, THE SAIL

CANOPUS

Canopus (Alpha Carinae) is a first magnitude star, the second brightest in the sky, and the brightest star in Carina, Puppis, and Vela. It is named after an ancient Greek navigator and is still used for space navigation today because it is bright and has few other bright stars nearby.

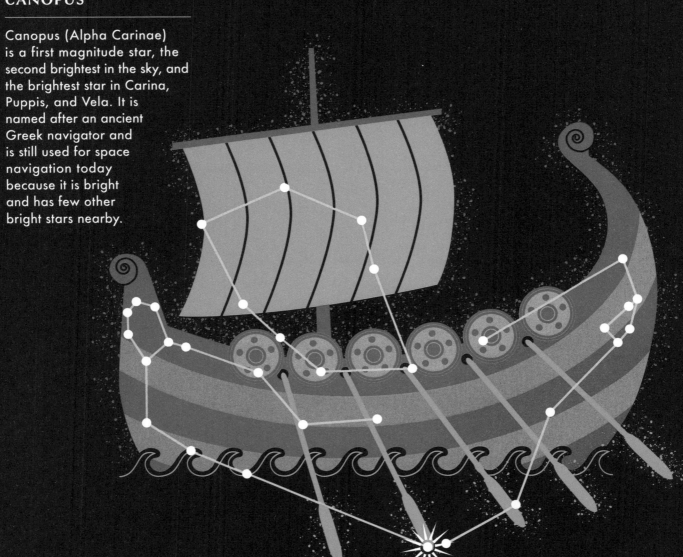

AURIGA

Auriga is a large constellation with many bright stars, whose main shape is an irregular hexagon, with a triangle at the top.

HOW TO FIND IT

Auriga is best seen between late Dec. and March from anywhere except the bottom half of the southern **hemisphere**.

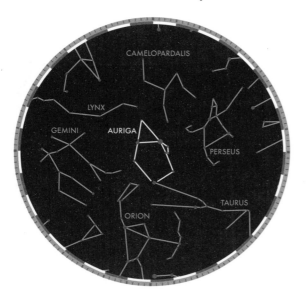

STORIES AND MYTHS

Auriga is Latin for "charioteer": a person who drives a chariot, which is a vehicle with two wheels pulled by horses. Many stories say that the charioteer is Erichthonius, a hero who was raised in Athens by the goddess Athena in ancient Greece. Athena taught Erichthonius to work with horses, which he mastered very quickly. His great knowledge of horses made him an excellent charioteer and helped him win many chariot races in the Panathenaic games: the Olympics of ancient Athens! Some stories say that he invented the *quadriga*: a chariot pulled by four horses, which really impressed **Zeus**. Some stories say that the goat in Auriga's arm is the goat that nursed Zeus as a baby — but no one really knows why the Charioteer is holding her!

THE CHARIOTEER

CAPELLA

Capella (Alpha Aurigae), which comes from the Roman word for "she-goat," is a first magnitude star, the sixth brightest in the sky, and the brightest star in Auriga. Although it looks like a single star, it's actually two pairs of stars, known as a double-double **star system**.

BOÖTES

Boötes is the 13th largest constellation in the sky and contains many bright stars. Its stars form a kite or ice-cream-cone shape.

HOW TO FIND IT

Boötes is best seen between late March and June from nearly everywhere on Earth where people live.

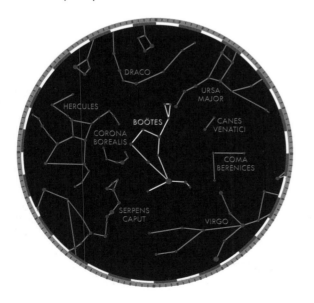

STORIES AND MYTHS

Boötes is also known as the Herdsman. He herds the Great Bear (Ursa Major) and the Little Bear (Ursa Minor) constellations around the sky, with the help of the two dogs in the constellation Canes Venatici. He stands right behind Ursa Major and is usually pictured carrying a sickle (a tool for farming) in one hand and a shepherd's staff in the other. Some stories say that the name Boötes comes from an ancient Greek word for "ox-driver" because the stars of the Great Bear (Ursa Major) were once pictured as oxen.

THE HERDSMAN

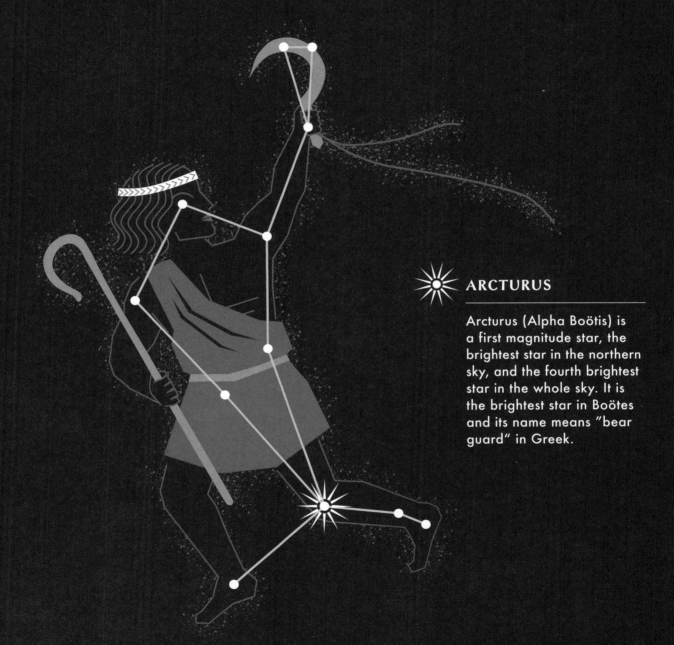

ARCTURUS

Arcturus (Alpha Boötis) is a first magnitude star, the brightest star in the northern sky, and the fourth brightest star in the whole sky. It is the brightest star in Boötes and its name means "bear guard" in Greek.

CANIS MAJOR

Canis Major is a medium-sized constellation whose stars connect to look very much like a dog. It also has the honor of being home to the brightest star in the entire sky: Sirius.

HOW TO FIND IT

Canis Major is best seen between late Dec. and March from nearly everywhere on Earth where people live.

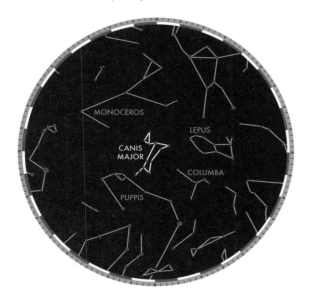

STORIES AND MYTHS

Canis Major, which means the "greater dog" in Latin, is said to be the guard dog of Orion, the hunter. It follows Orion around the sky. Some ancient Greek myths say that the dog is Laelaps, the fastest dog in the world, which always caught what it hunted. King Cephalus sent it after the Teumissian fox, a mythical animal that could never be caught. They chased each other for years, and when there was no end to the chase in sight, **Zeus** froze them both, and placed Laelaps in the sky as Canis Major.

THE GREATER DOG

SIRIUS

Sirius (Alpha Canis Majoris) was called the Dog Star long before the constellation Canis Major existed. The name Sirius comes from a Greek word that means "scorching," because the ancient Greeks noticed how Sirius would rise at the same time as the Sun only during the hottest days of the summer. Many of us today still refer to this sizzling time of year as the "dog days!"

CANIS MINOR

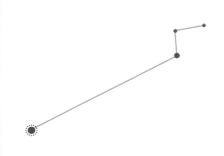

LOCATION: EQUATORIAL

Canis Minor is one of the smallest constellations. Its stars make a simple bent-line shape.

HOW TO FIND IT

Canis Minor is best seen between late Dec. and March from nearly everywhere on Earth where people live.

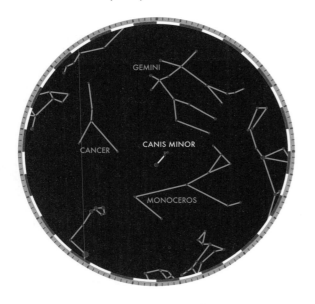

STORIES AND MYTHS

Canis Minor, which means the "lesser dog" in Latin, follows and guards Orion along with Canis Major. Some stories say that this dog is Maera, who was the very loyal pet dog of Icarius, a man from Athens. When Icarius died, Maera was so sad that Icarius's good friend, the god Dionysus, placed it in the sky next to the heavenly river, the **Milky Way**, where it would never be thirsty. Other stories say that Canis Minor may have originally been the Teumissian fox, a mythical animal that could never be caught. When Laelaps, the dog that always caught what it hunted (represented by Canis Major), was sent after the fox, **Zeus** put a stop to the chase by freezing them both in the sky.

THE LESSER DOG

PROCYON

Procyon (Alpha Canis Minoris) is a first magnitude star, the eighth brightest in the sky, and the brightest star in Canis Minor. The word Procyon comes from a Greek word for "before the dog" because the star rises before Sirius (as seen from the Mediterreanean lands).

CASSIOPEIA

Cassiopeia is an important constellation that is small but bright, with a shape that's easy to remember. It is shaped like an M or W, depending on the time of year.

HOW TO FIND IT

Cassiopeia is best seen between late Sept. and Dec. from the northern **hemisphere** and the north of the southern hemisphere.

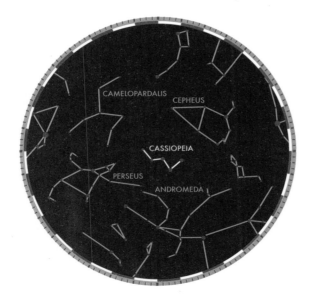

STORIES AND MYTHS

In Greek mythology, Cassiopeia was a queen of Ethiopia who cared a lot about looks, and spent a lot of time thinking (and bragging!) about her beauty and that of her daughter, Andromeda. She is often pictured sitting on her royal throne, looking at herself in a mirror, and brushing or smoothing her long hair. Cassiopeia's bragging almost cost the life of her daughter, and her story was a reminder to the ancient Greeks that it is better to put energy into kindness than beauty and looks.

THE SEATED QUEEN

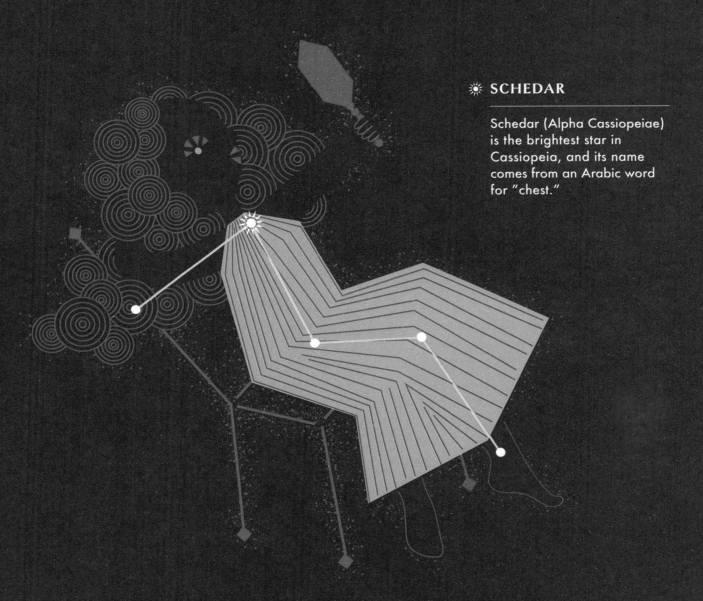

☀ **SCHEDAR**

Schedar (Alpha Cassiopeiae) is the brightest star in Cassiopeia, and its name comes from an Arabic word for "chest."

CENTAURUS

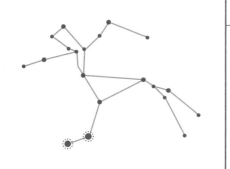

Centaurus is the ninth-largest constellation in the sky, and is home to many bright and easy-to-find stars. Its two brightest stars are called the Pointers because they can be used to help find the **south celestial pole**, which is an imaginary point in the sky just above the South Pole.

HOW TO FIND IT

Centaurus is best seen between late March and June in the southern **hemisphere** and the south of the northern hemisphere.

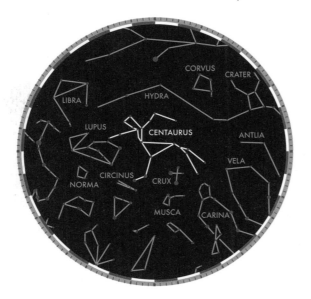

STORIES AND MYTHS

A **centaur** is a mythical creature with the head and torso of a man and the legs of a horse. Centaurus is based on a special centaur in Greek mythology named Chiron. While centaurs had a reputation for being wild and behaving badly, Chiron was very wise, kind, and clever. He was so admired that many of the greatest heroes in Greek myths were sent to him to be taught and trained in archery, hunting, physical fitness, the healing arts, and music. Sadly, Chiron was accidentally shot by Hercules with a poisoned arrow, but he was honored by being placed in the sky.

THE CENTAUR

HADAR

Hadar (Beta Centauri) is a first magnitude star, the 11th brightest in the sky, and the second brightest in Centaurus. Its name comes from the Arabic word for "on the ground."

ALPHA CENTAURI

Alpha Centauri looks like one star, but is actually a group of three stars that **orbit** one another, known as a triple **star system**. Together, it appears as a first magnitude star, the third brightest in the sky, and the brightest in Centaurus. It is sometimes called Rigil Kentaurus, which comes from an Arabic word for "centaur's foot."

CEPHEUS

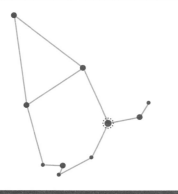

Cepheus is not as bright and easy to see as some of the other constellations around it, but its stars make a house shape, which makes it easy to find. It sits next to Cassiopeia in the sky.

HOW TO FIND IT

It is best seen between late Sept. and Dec. from the northern **hemisphere** and just below the **equator** in the southern hemisphere.

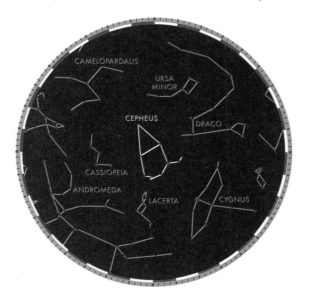

STORIES AND MYTHS

Cepheus was a king of ancient Ethiopia, and the unfortunate husband of Cassiopeia, whose family was punished when she bragged about the beauty of her daughter, Andromeda. When the sea god, Poseidon, sent the terrible sea monster, Cetus, to terrorize Ethiopia's coastline, Cepheus did not know how to get rid of Cetus, so he consulted an **oracle**, a person who can tell the future. The oracle told him that the only way to stop the sea monster was to sacrifice his daughter to it. Most fathers wouldn't imagine doing so, but Cepheus chained his daughter to a rock by the ocean and left her to be taken by the monster. Luckily, the hero, Perseus, helped her!

THE KING

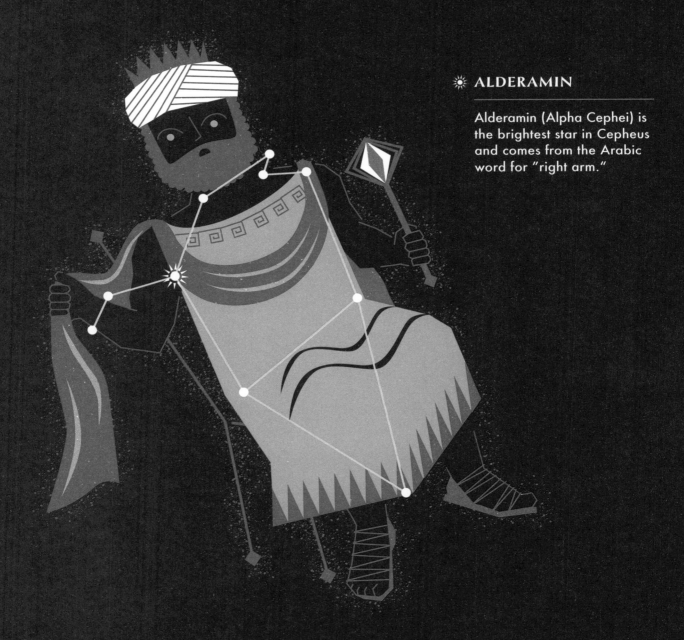

☀ **ALDERAMIN**

Alderamin (Alpha Cephei) is the brightest star in Cepheus and comes from the Arabic word for "right arm."

CETUS

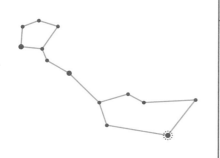

LOCATION: EQUATORIAL

Cetus is the fourth-largest constellation in the sky, but it is not as bright as some of the others. It has a small loop on one end and a larger loop on the other, connected by a jagged line.

HOW TO FIND IT

Cetus is best seen between late Sept. and Dec. from nearly everywhere on Earth where people live.

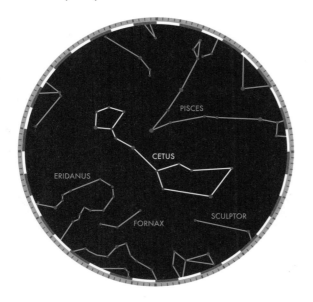

STORIES AND MYTHS

Cetus is often referred to as the Whale, but the ancient Greeks knew this creature as a sea monster or sea dragon, with small paws, the head of a dog, and the body of a sea creature. Cetus was sent by Poseidon, the god of the sea, to demolish the coast of ancient Ethiopia as a punishment for King Cepheus and his family. Just as Cetus was about to kill the princess Andromeda, the hero Perseus arrived and killed Cetus. Some stories say that Perseus used a sword to slay Cetus, while others say that he used the head of **Medusa**, a monster with serpents for hair whose face could turn anyone who looked at it to stone.

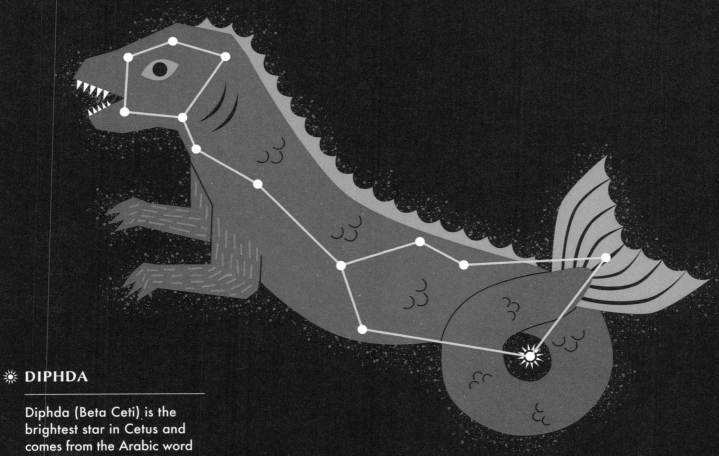

☀ DIPHDA

Diphda (Beta Ceti) is the brightest star in Cetus and comes from the Arabic word for "frog."

COMA BERENICES

LOCATION: NORTHERN HEMISPHERE

Coma Berenices is a medium-sized constellation that forms a simple right angle.

HOW TO FIND IT

Coma Berenices is best seen between late March and June from nearly everywhere on Earth where people live.

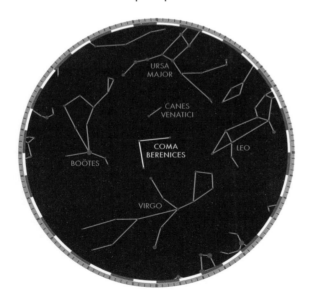

STORIES AND MYTHS

Coma Berenices, which means "Berenice's hair" in Latin, is one of the few constellations to be named after a real person. Queen Berenice the Second ruled Egypt with King Ptolemy the Third thousands of years ago. She was known as a brave warrior who also had extremely long and beautiful hair. When her husband left for war, Berenice vowed that if he came back safely she would make an offering to the gods by cutting off her hair in gratitude. Ptolemy returned, and Berenice cut off her locks and placed them on an altar. The next day, her precious sacrifice was nowhere to be found until it was spotted by the court's astronomer, tucked away safely up in the stars.

BERENICE'S HAIR

☀ **BETA COMAE BERENICES**

Beta Comae Berenices is the brightest star in Coma Berenices. It is sometimes called al-Dafira, which comes from an Arabic word for "lock" or "braid" of hair.

CORONA AUSTRALIS

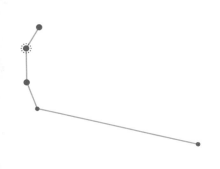

Corona Australis is a very small constellation whose stars form an easy-to-find shape that looks a bit like a hook.

HOW TO FIND IT

It is best seen between late June and Sept. from the southern **hemisphere** and the bottom half of the northern hemisphere.

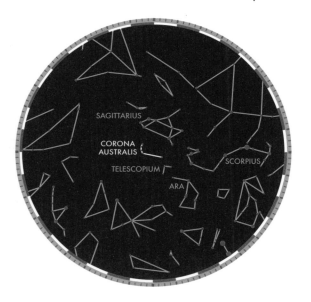

STORIES AND MYTHS

Corona Australis, which is Latin for "southern crown," is usually pictured as a wreath made of laurel branches or myrtle leaves. In ancient Greece, wreaths symbolized victory and honor, and were worn on the head like a crown. Some stories claim that this wreath belonged to either Centaurus or Sagittarius because it sits near them in the sky. Other stories say that the crown came from Dionysus, the **demigod** son of **Zeus** and the **mortal** woman named Semele. Dionysus placed a crown of myrtle leaves in the sky to honor his mother's rescue from Hades, the underworld.

THE SOUTHERN CROWN

☀ **ALPHA CORONAE AUSTRALIS**

Alpha Coronae Australis is the brightest star in Corona Australis. It is sometimes called Alphekka Meridiana, which comes from an Arabic phrase: "the bright (star) of the broken ring (of stars)."

CORONA BOREALIS

LOCATION: NORTHERN HEMISPHERE

Corona Borealis is a very small constellation, whose stars form a semicircle or hook shape.

HOW TO FIND IT

Corona Borealis is best seen between late June and Sept. from anywhere except the very bottom of the southern **hemisphere**.

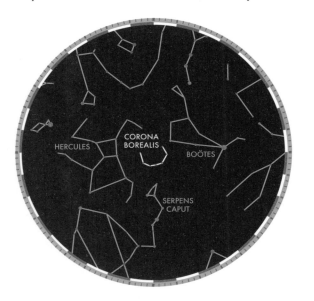

STORIES AND MYTHS

In ancient Greek mythology, the Northern Crown, or Corona Borealis in Latin, was the crown that Princess Ariadne of Crete wore when she married Dionysus, the god of wine-making and festivals. The crown was set with sparkling gems, and some stories say that it was created by Hephaestus, the god of fire. After the wedding, Dionysus threw the crown up into the sky in celebration, where its jewels turned into stars.

THE NORTHERN CROWN

☀ **ALPHEKKA**

Alphekka (Alpha Coronae Borealis) is the brightest star in Corona Borealis. Like Alphekka Meridiana in the Southern Crown, its name also means the "bright (star) of the broken ring (of stars)," though it is a completely different star.

CORVUS AND CRATER

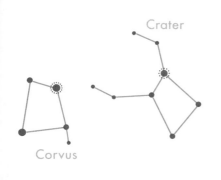

Crater

Corvus

LOCATION: SOUTHERN HEMISPHERE

Corvus and Crater are two small constellations that sit next to each other above Hydra, the water snake. The stars in Corvus and Crater are not very bright, but are in a dark area of the sky, which makes them easy to find.

HOW TO FIND IT

Corvus and Crater are best seen between late March and June from nearly everywhere on Earth where people live.

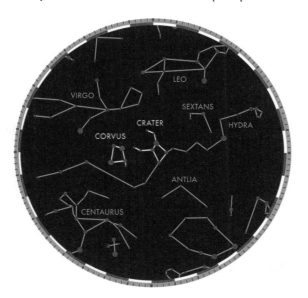

STORIES AND MYTHS

Corvus, which is Latin for "crow," and Crater, Latin for "cup," are part of an ancient Greek moral tale. One day, the god Apollo was preparing a **sacrifice** to **Zeus** and asked the crow to bring him water. The crow flew off with a goblet-like cup in its beak, but on its way, spotted a tree full of almost-ripe figs. The crow ended up waiting days for them to ripen so it could eat them, and returned empty-handed to Apollo. It blamed Hydra, a water monster, for blocking the spring, but Apollo could see that the crow was lying, so he punished it by making it permanently thirsty. Corvus sits up in the sky, the cup of water beside it, always just out of reach, which may explain why crows have a raspy caw!

THE CROW AND THE CUP

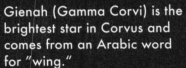

☀ GIENAH

Gienah (Gamma Corvi) is the brightest star in Corvus and comes from an Arabic word for "wing."

☀ DELTA CRATERIS

Delta Crateris is the brightest star in Crater.

CYGNUS

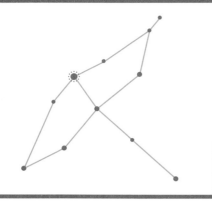

LOCATION: NORTHERN HEMISPHERE

Cygnus is a large constellation and its stars form a very big cross shape. It contains an **asterism** called the Northern Cross.

HOW TO FIND IT

Cygnus is best seen between late June and Sept. from anywhere except the bottom half of the southern **hemisphere**.

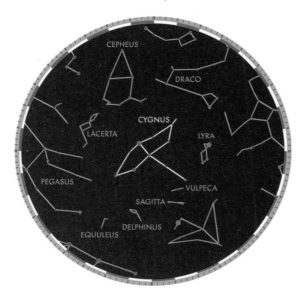

STORIES AND MYTHS

Cygnus, which means "swan" in Latin, is associated with several different Greek myths. In one myth, the friends Cycnus, the son of Poseidon, and Phaethon, the **mortal** son of the sun god Helios, were racing their chariots in the sky. When they drove too close to the Sun, the chariots burned up, and Phaethon fell from the sky into a river and died. Cycnus was so devastated by the loss of his good friend that **Zeus** took pity on him, turned him into a swan, and placed him among the stars.

THE SWAN

DENEB

Deneb (Alpha Cygni) is a first magnitude star, the 20th brightest in the sky, and the brightest star in Cygnus. Its name comes from an Arabic word for "tail."

ASTERISM

Northern Cross

DELPHINUS

LOCATION: NORTHERN HEMISPHERE

Delphinus is one of the smaller constellations in the sky, but is easy to find because its bright stars form a diamond shape with a line at the bottom, a bit like a kite. It is home to the **asterism** Job's Coffin.

HOW TO FIND IT

Delphinus is best seen between late June and Sept. from nearly everywhere on Earth where people live.

STORIES AND MYTHS

Delphinus means "dolphin" in Latin, and dolphins were a very common sight for the ancient Greeks, who believed that they carried messages for Poseidon, the god of the sea. When Poseidon fell in love with a sea goddess, he sent a kind and gentle dolphin to visit her and convince her to marry him. In another story, a famous Greek poet and musician, Arion, escaped robbers at sea by attracting a school of dolphins with his music. He was carried back home by a friendly dolphin, which was placed in the sky by Apollo, the god of music and poetry. Delphinus sits near Arion's famous lyre in the constellation Lyra.

THE DOLPHIN

Job's Coffin

☀ BETA DELPHINI

Beta Delphini is the brightest star in Delphinus, and is sometimes called Rotanev, a name that has a secret code in it! The star above it, Alpha Delphini, is sometimes called Sualocin. If you read these two names together backward, they spell "Nicolaus Venator," the Latin name of an Italian astronomer from the 1800s.

DRACO

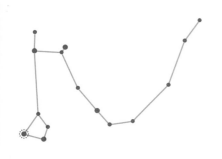

LOCATION: NORTHERN HEMISPHERE

Draco is the eighth-largest constellation in the sky. Its stars form an irregular **polygon** with a long winding line that curves around the **north celestial pole**, an imaginary point in the sky directly above Earth's north pole.

HOW TO FIND IT

Draco is best seen between late June and Sept. from the northern **hemisphere** and the northern parts of the southern hemisphere.

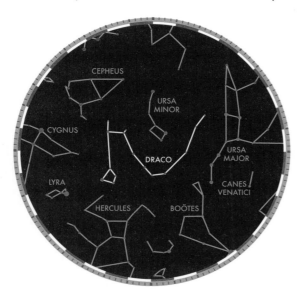

STORIES AND MYTHS

Zeus's wife, Hera, had a precious apple tree that was given to her as a wedding present when she married Zeus. It was so special that she had it guarded by a vicious, snake like dragon named Ladon. The apples were golden, and whoever was lucky enough to eat one became **immortal**! One day the hero Hercules visited the tree in order to complete one of the 12 tasks (or labors) he'd been given to make up for a terrible crime he had committed. He was able to complete his task — stealing some of the tree's golden apples — by slaying the dragon with a poison arrow. Hera placed the image of her dragon in the sky as the constellation Draco.

THE DRAGON

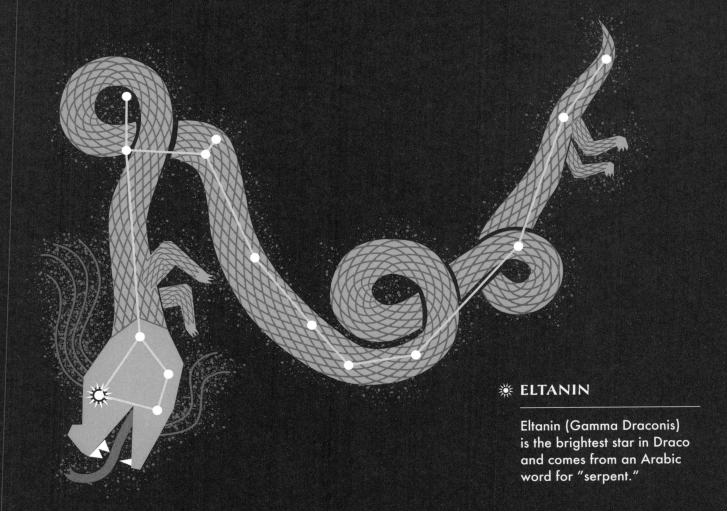

☀ **ELTANIN**

Eltanin (Gamma Draconis) is the brightest star in Draco and comes from an Arabic word for "serpent."

EQUULEUS

LOCATION: NORTHERN HEMISPHERE

Equuleus is the second-smallest constellation in the sky. Its stars make a line with a bent angle.

HOW TO FIND IT

Equuleus is best seen between late June and Sept. from nearly everywhere on Earth where people live.

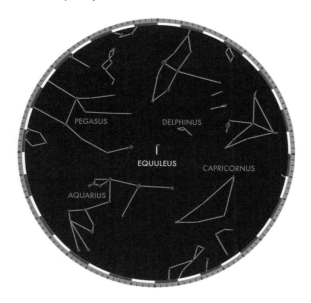

STORIES AND MYTHS

The little horse — *equuleus* in Latin — sits next to Pegasus, and some stories say that he is Pegasus's son or brother Celeris, which means "swiftness" or "speed" in Latin. Other stories say that this little horse represents Hippe, the daughter of the **centaur** Chiron (represented by the constellation Centaurus). Hippe fell in love with someone Chiron did not approve of, and fled to the mountains to hide from her father. When he came looking for her, the gods took pity on her and changed her into a mare, or female horse. It is said that Artemis, the goddess of the hunt and protector of young girls, placed the image of Hippe among the stars, where she still hides from Chiron, with only her head showing.

THE LITTLE HORSE

☀ KITALPHA

Kitalpha (Alpha Equulei) is the brightest star in Equuleus and comes from an Arabic word for "a piece of the horse."

ERIDANUS

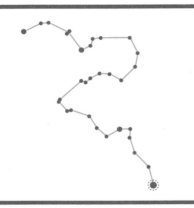

LOCATION: EQUATORIAL

Eridanus is one of the largest constellations in the sky, and its stars make a long, curving line, like a flowing river.

HOW TO FIND IT

Eridanus is best seen between late Dec. and March from the southern **hemisphere**, and the lower third of the northern hemisphere.

STORIES AND MYTHS

Rivers made life possible in the ancient world by providing water that was important for farming and daily life. So it is no surprise that ancient Babylonians first pictured a river in these stars, or that the ancient Greeks saw magical power in the river's flowing waters. Some stories associate Eridanus with a myth about Phaethon, son of Helios, the Greek sun god. Phaethon begged to ride his father's chariot, drove too close to the Sun, then crashed and burned, landing in this river.

THE RIVER

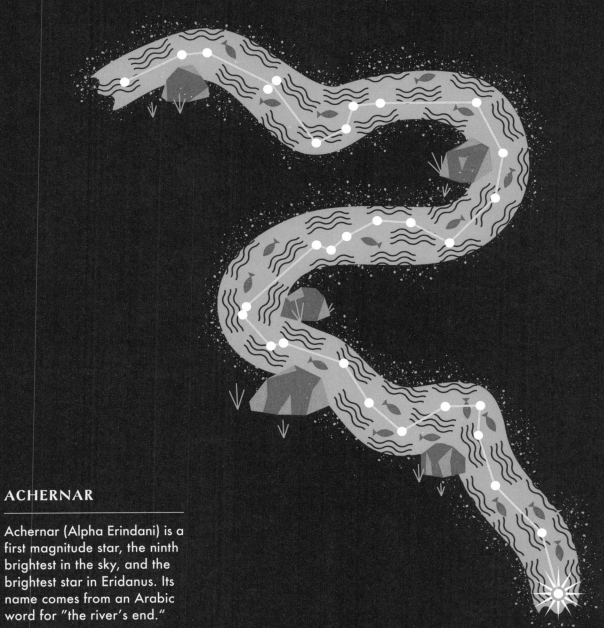

ACHERNAR

Achernar (Alpha Erindani) is a first magnitude star, the ninth brightest in the sky, and the brightest star in Eridanus. Its name comes from an Arabic word for "the river's end."

HERCULES

Hercules is the fifth-largest constellation in the sky. Its stars make the shape of a kneeling person. In fact, before this constellation was associated with Hercules, it was simply called the Kneeling One.

HOW TO FIND IT

Hercules is best seen between late June and Sept. from anywhere except for the southern part of the southern **hemisphere**.

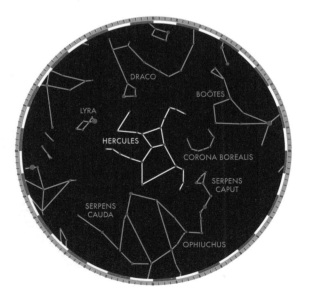

STORIES AND MYTHS

Hercules, or Heracles in Greek, was the most well-known and strongest hero character in ancient mythology. This half-god half-**mortal** is most famous for his 12 labors — the 12 tasks he had to complete to pay for a crime he'd committed. These included killing the invincible Nemean lion, destroying the many-headed sea monster Hydra, and sneaking past the snake like dragon Ladon to steal the golden apples of immortality from Hera's garden. Although these tasks were thought to be impossible, he achieved all 12 using his incredible strength, skill, and bravery. After he paid for his mistakes, he was given a place among the **gods of Mount Olympus**.

HERCULES

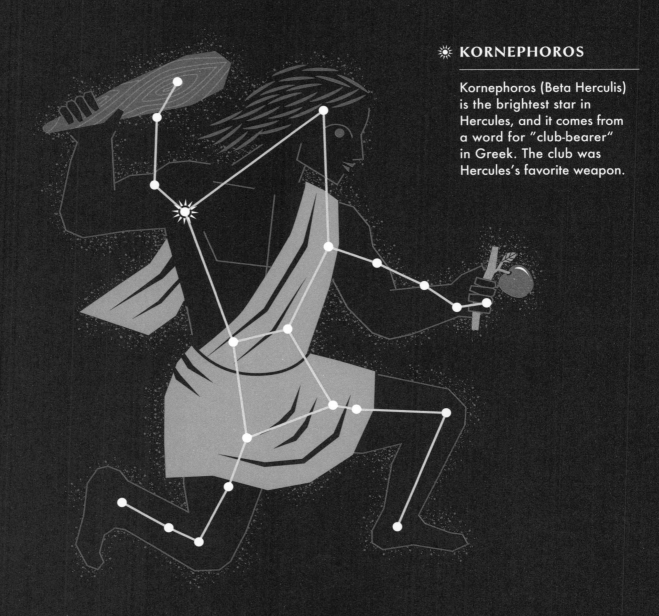

☀ **KORNEPHOROS**

Kornephoros (Beta Herculis) is the brightest star in Hercules, and it comes from a word for "club-bearer" in Greek. The club was Hercules's favorite weapon.

HYDRA

LOCATION: EQUATORIAL

Hydra is the largest constellation, covering one quarter of the sky, although it doesn't have a lot of bright stars. It makes a twisting line, with a small irregular **polygon** at the top, like a snake's head.

HOW TO FIND IT

Hydra is best seen between late March and June from nearly anywhere except for the north and south polar regions.

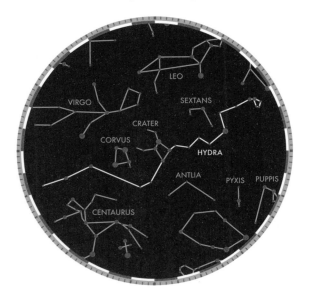

STORIES AND MYTHS

The water snake, *hydra* in Latin, is best known as the sea serpent who Hercules had to fight in the second of his famous tasks. Hydra was the half-sister of Ladon, the snake like beast who guarded Hera's golden apples. She lived in a swamp, and was so wretched that even her breath could kill someone. Hydra supposedly had nine heads, of which the middle one was **immortal**. In the sky, she is usually shown with one head only — possibly her immortal one! After Hydra was killed by Hercules, he made poison-tipped arrows from her toxic blood, which he later used to fight Ladon in his second-to-last task. Hydra also appears in the story of Corvus, the crow, as the snake who the crow blamed for blocking the spring.

THE WATER SNAKE

☀ ALPHARD

Alphard (Alpha Hydrae) is the brightest star in Hydra and its name means "the solitary one" in Arabic.

LEPUS

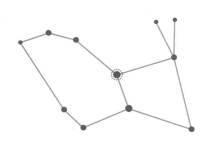

LOCATION: SOUTHERN HEMISPHERE

Lepus is a medium-sized constellation whose stars form a shape that looks a lot like a rabbit.

HOW TO FIND IT

Lepus is best seen between late Dec. through March from nearly everywhere on Earth where people live.

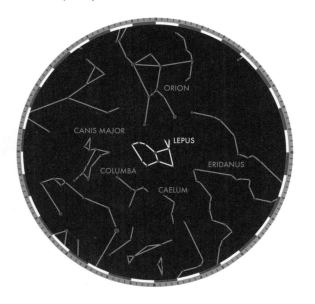

STORIES AND MYTHS

A hare is like a rabbit, only it's larger and faster. Lepus, which means "hare" in Latin, is very easy to confuse with the constellation Lupus, which means "wolf"! This hare sits near Orion, the hunter, and his dogs, Canis Major and Canis Minor, and looks as if it is being chased by them. But don't worry, since they rotate around the sky together, Orion and his dogs will never catch it! Hermes, the messenger of the Greek gods, put this hare in the sky precisely because it was so speedy!

THE HARE

☀ **ARNEB**

Arneb (Alpha Leporis) is the brightest star in Lepus and its name comes from an Arabic word for "hare."

LUPUS

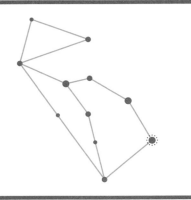

Lupus is a smaller constellation whose stars make the shape of a seated dog like animal.

HOW TO FIND IT

Lupus is best seen between late March and June from the southern **hemisphere** and the lower third of the northern hemisphere.

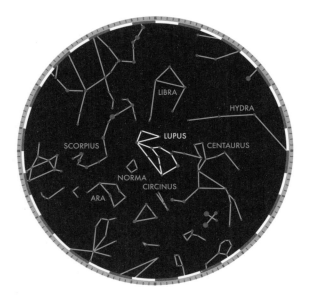

STORIES AND MYTHS

The stars of Lupus, which is Latin for "wolf," used to be combined with the constellation Centaurus as an animal being offered to the gods. Lupus now stands alone as a free animal, and although this constellation represented a "mad dog" to the Babylonians, a "wild animal" to the Greeks, and simply a "beast" to the Romans, it became known as a wolf many hundreds of years later when the constellation stories were translated into Latin.

THE WOLF

✹ ALPHA LUPI

Alpha Lupi is the brightest star in Lupus, and it is 10 times larger than the Sun!

LYRA

Lyra is a small but bright constellation whose stars form two **polygons** that make a shape that looks like a number eight.

HOW TO FIND IT

Lyra is best seen from late June to Sept. from anywhere except the lower third of the southern **hemisphere**.

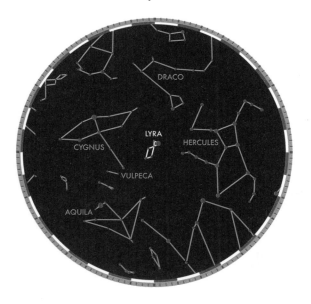

STORIES AND MYTHS

The lyre — *lyra* in Latin — is a stringed instrument that sounds a bit like a guitar or a harp. This mythical lyre was created by the god Hermes out of a tortoise shell and given to Orpheus, a legendary musician whose music was magical. His songs were so bewitching that they could move nature: rivers could be tamed, arrows could be redirected, and trees uprooted themselves to follow him. Orpheus traveled with captain Jason aboard the *Argo* during his quest for the Golden Fleece. When they heard Sirens — bird like creatures who used their songs to lure sailors into danger — Orpheus played his lyre, drowning out the Sirens' song with his powerful music and keeping the ship's sailors safe. When Orpheus died, **Zeus** put his lyre in the heavens.

THE LYRE

VEGA

Vega (Alpha Lyrae) is a
first magnitude star, the fifth
brightest in the sky, and the
brightest star in Lyra. Its
name comes from "vulture"
in Arabic, because the
Arabs originally pictured
this constellation as a bird
swooping on its prey.

ORION

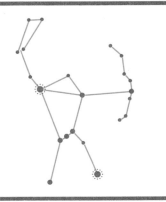

LOCATION: EQUATORIAL

Orion is one of the best-known constellations in the sky and easy to find because it has some of the brightest and most distinctive stars in the sky. Orion contains two very well-known **asterisms**: Orion's Belt and Orion's Sword.

HOW TO FIND IT

Orion is best seen between late Dec. and March from nearly everywhere on Earth where people live.

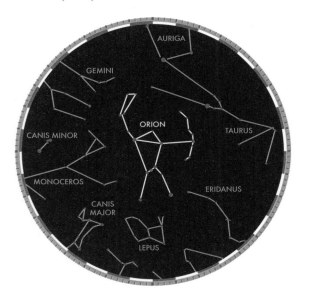

STORIES AND MYTHS

Orion, the son of the sea god Poseidon, was a hunter who was unusually tall, handsome, and strong. One day Orion went hunting with Artemis, goddess of the hunt, and bragged about how he could kill every animal on Earth if he wanted to. This made **Gaia**, the earth goddess, so angry that she sent a giant scorpion, Scorpius, to kill him. Both Orion and the scorpion were placed among the constellations as a warning to others not to upset Gaia. Orion has his trusted hunting dogs, Canis Major and Canis Minor, behind him in the sky to help and protect him.

BETELGEUSE

Betelgeuse (Alpha Orionis)
is a first magnitude star, the
10th brightest star in the sky,
and the second brightest
star in Orion. Its name is
pronounced Be-tel-juice and
comes from an Arabic word
that means both "the hand
of Orion" and "the giant's
shoulder."

RIGEL

Rigel (Beta Orionis) is also
a first magnitude star, the
seventh brightest in the sky,
and the brightest star in
Orion. Its name comes from
an Arabic word for "foot."

ASTERISMS

Orion's
Belt

Orion's
Sword

PEGASUS

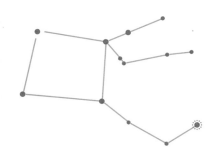

Pegasus is one of the largest constellations in the sky, whose brightest stars, when combined with one of the stars from its neighboring constellation, Andromeda, form a square shape that is an **asterism** called the Great Square of Pegasus.

HOW TO FIND IT

Pegasus is best seen between late Sept. and Dec. from nearly anywhere except the bottom third of the southern **hemisphere**.

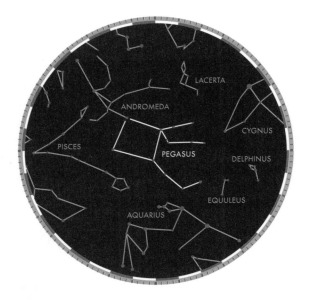

STORIES AND MYTHS

Pegasus was a winged horse that is said to have been the child of a surprising combination of parents: Poseidon, god of the sea, and **Medusa**, a winged monster with snakes for hair. Wherever Pegasus's hooves touched the ground, water would magically spring up. In fact, Pegasus comes from a Greek word for "springs." Pegasus is best known for helping great heroes such as Perseus, who rescued the princess Andromeda, and Bellerophon, who killed the fire-breathing, three-headed monster Chimera. Later, Pegasus lived in the gods' stables on **Mount Olympus** and delivered thunderbolts for **Zeus**.

THE WINGED HORSE

Enif (Epsilon Pegasi) comes from the Arabic for "nose" and is the brightest star in Pegasus.

ASTERISM

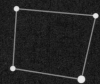

Great Square
of Pegasus

PERSEUS

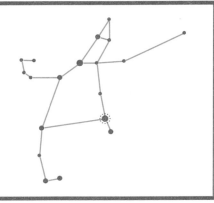

LOCATION: NORTHERN HEMISPHERE

Perseus is a medium-sized constellation whose stars form the shape of a person holding a sword. It is also home to the star Algol, which some people think is unlucky or scary because of the way its light changes in brightness.

HOW TO FIND IT

Perseus is best seen between late Sept. and Dec. from the northern **hemisphere**.

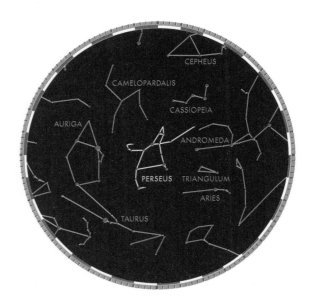

STORIES AND MYTHS

Perseus was the son of **Zeus** and the princess Danae. He is famous in Greek mythology for his many heroic acts. He defeated the snake-haired monster, **Medusa**, who had a face that would turn anyone who looked at it to stone, and rescued the princess Andromeda from the vicious sea monster Cetus. Perseus sits in the sky beside his love, Andromeda, whom he later married, and close to other characters from his life story, such as Cassiopeia and Cepheus.

PERSEUS

☀ ALGOL

Algol (Beta Persei) is the second-brightest but most well-known star in Perseus. Its name comes from an Arabic word for "demon," and it usually marks the head of Medusa.

PISCIS AUSTRINUS

LOCATION: SOUTHERN HEMISPHERE

Piscis Austrinus is a small but bright constellation whose stars make a very fish like shape.

HOW TO FIND IT

It is best seen between late Sept. and Dec. from the southern **hemisphere** and the lower half of the northern hemisphere.

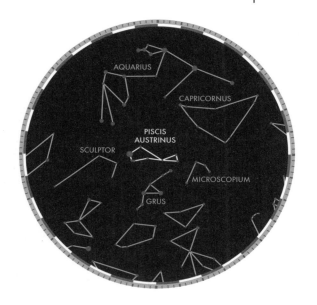

STORIES AND MYTHS

Piscis Austrinus, which means "southern fish" in Latin, was pictured in many ancient cultures as — you guessed it — a fish! The Greeks called it the Great Fish and some considered it the parent of the two fish in the constellation Pisces. The Southern Fish sits just below the constellation of Aquarius, and is often pictured under the flow of water from Aquarius's cup, as though it's drinking from it.

THE SOUTHERN FISH

FOMALHAUT

Fomalhaut (Alpha Piscis Austrini) is a first magnitude star, the 18th brightest in the sky, and the brightest star in Piscis Austrinus. Its name comes from an Arabic word for "the mouth of the whale."

SAGITTA

LOCATION: NORTHERN HEMISPHERE

Sagitta is the third-smallest constellation in the sky. Its stars form the shape of a line with a narrow V at the end, which looks a lot like an arrow. Because of its distinctive shape, it has been seen as an arrow by many cultures.

HOW TO FIND IT

Sagitta is best seen between late June and Sept. from nearly everywhere on Earth where people live.

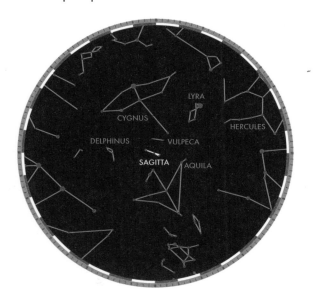

STORIES AND MYTHS

You might think that this arrow — *sagitta* in Latin — belongs to Sagittarius, the archer, but it doesn't! None of the myths and stories connect Sagitta to Sagittarius. Instead, it is known as the arrow that Hercules used to kill the eagle that was sent by **Zeus** to punish the **immortal Titan** Prometheus. He had stolen the idea of fire from the gods and given it to humans, which angered the gods. Prometheus was tied to a rock and an eagle was sent to peck at him every day as punishment. Thankfully, Hercules used his arrow to set Prometheus free.

THE ARROW

SERPENS

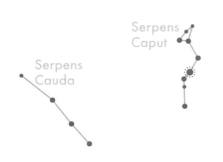

Serpens Caput

Serpens Cauda

Serpens is a large constellation, and its stars make a winding, curving line shape. It is divided into two parts: Serpens Caput (Latin for "serpent's head") and Serpens Cauda (Latin for "serpent's tail"), which sit on either side of the constellation Ophiuchus.

HOW TO FIND IT

Serpens is best seen between late June and Sept. from nearly everywhere on Earth where people live.

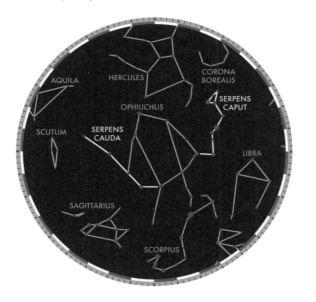

STORIES AND MYTHS

Serpens, which means "the snake" in Latin, is usually pictured being held up by Asclepius, the god of medicine, shown in the constellation Ophiuchus. Asclepius once saw a snake bring another dead snake back to life by placing a healing herb on it. He was so impressed, that he tried the snake's technique on a man who had died. The herb worked and the man miraculously came back to life! The Rod of Asclepius, which is an image of a staff or rod with one single snake wrapped around it, is often still used to symbolize medicine and healing. It is even used in the logo for the World Health Organization!

THE SERPENT

☀ **UNUKALHAI**

Unukalhai (Alpha Serpentis) comes from Arabic for the "serpent's neck."

TRIANGULUM

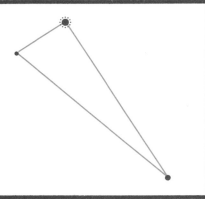

LOCATION: NORTHERN HEMISPHERE

Triangulum is one of the smallest constellations in the sky and its stars make — you guessed it — a triangle shape!

HOW TO FIND IT

Triangulum is best seen between late Sept. and Dec. from nearly everywhere on Earth where people live.

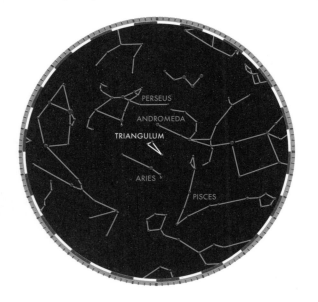

STORIES AND MYTHS

Triangulum, which means "triangle" in Latin, was once called Deltoton because it looked like the Greek letter delta, which is also shaped like a triangle: Δ. Other people looked up into the sky and saw a shape that looked like the Nile River Delta, or the island of Sicily, which are also shaped a bit like a triangle.

THE TRIANGLE

☀ **BETA TRIANGULI**

Beta Trianguli is the brightest star in Triangulum.

URSA MAJOR

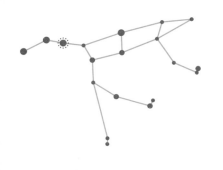

LOCATION: NORTHERN HEMISPHERE

Ursa Major is the third-largest constellation in the sky and is very old. One of the most famous **asterisms** in the sky is found in Ursa Major: the Big Dipper. The two front stars in this asterism are called Pointers. They point to Polaris (the North Star).

HOW TO FIND IT

Ursa Major is best seen between late March and June in the northern **hemisphere** and the top third of the southern hemisphere.

STORIES AND MYTHS

Ursa Major is Latin for "greater she-bear." Many different cultures have imagined a bear in this group of stars! Due to their positions near the **north celestial pole**, Boötes the Herdsman and his dogs follow the Great Bear around the sky all year round. In Greek mythology, Ursa Major was said to be Callisto, the huntress who gave birth to **Zeus's** son, whom she named Arcas. When Zeus's wife, Hera, found out, she was very angry and turned Callisto into a bear. Callisto wandered the forest, hiding from other hunters until Zeus later placed her safely up among the stars.

THE GREAT BEAR

☀ ALIOTH

Alioth (Epsilon Ursae Majoris) comes from an Arabic word for "fat tail of a sheep" and is the brightest star in Ursa Major.

ASTERISM

Big Dipper

URSA MINOR

Ursa Minor is a small but easy-to-see constellation whose stars make up the shape of a small ladle. It's also known as an **asterism** called the Little Dipper. Ursa Minor is home to one of the most important stars in the sky for navigation: Polaris, the North Star.

HOW TO FIND IT

It is best seen between late March and June in the northern **hemisphere** and just below the **equator** in the southern hemisphere.

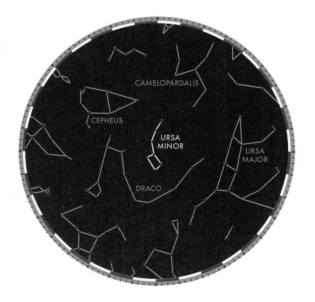

STORIES AND MYTHS

Even though it is not as big or bright as the Great Bear, the Little Bear — or Ursa Minor — has been very useful to many cultures for navigation because it does not move around like the other constellations as it is found at the **north celestial pole**. If sailors could find the Little Bear, they would know which direction was north. Greek mythology says that the Little Bear is Callisto's son, Arcas, who grew up to become a hunter. One day he came across his mother in bear form in the forest. Just as he was about to shoot her with an arrow, **Zeus** transformed him into a bear, too, and placed mother and son together among the stars.

THE LITTLE BEAR

☀ POLARIS

Polaris (Alpha Ursae Minoris) is the brightest star in Ursa Minor and the closest bright star to the north celestial pole. It is a very useful star for navigation, because it stays still while other stars around it move. When you are looking at Polaris, you are facing north.

THE MODERN CONSTELLATIONS

Can you imagine something that was discovered or named hundreds of years ago being labeled as "modern"? And yet constellations that were created and mapped in the 1600s are often referred to in that way. Astronomers during that century lived during a time when many exciting inventions were being built. Several of these inventions made a big difference to people studying the stars: telescopes, navigational tools, and larger, faster ships. Telescopes allowed them to see stars that, until then, were too faint to see with the naked eye. Navigational tools — such as the octant and sextant — and bigger ships allowed them to travel to parts of the world where they could chart stars they hadn't seen before.

This era is known as the Age of Exploration, and Europeans explored the land, sea, and sky extensively. Astronomers saw that there were still many areas of the sky that didn't contain officially mapped constellations, so they set out to find as many stars as they could, and connect them into pictures. They wanted to make as complete a map of the sky as possible. Some constellations were introduced that related to the ancient ones: for example, Leo Minor is a baby lion to the larger constellation Leo, and Canes Venatici are the hunting dogs of Boötes the Herdsman. But not all the new pictures were inspired by ancient myths and legends.

Astronomers also created and introduced many constellations that were inspired by the time they lived in, and by the places they traveled to on their explorations. Sailing to the shores of Australia or Indonesia, for example, exposed them to fascinating animals they had never seen before, such as the chameleon and the toucan. New constellations were also named after the scientific instruments that helped them so much, including the octant, sextant, and the telescope.

ANIMALS AND PEOPLE

Birds of paradise, flying fish, and toucans do not live in the Netherlands, Poland, or France, so the sight of these exotic creatures must have amazed and inspired the European explorers who were charting constellations. Astronomers named constellations after many animals they would have found in places they traveled to, such as Papua New Guinea, South Asia, and Southeast Asia. They even named constellations after animals that they hadn't seen, as well as mythical animals, such as the phoenix and the unicorn!

These astronomers include the Dutch explorers Pieter Dirkzoon Keyser and Frederick de Houtman, who traveled together in the late 1500s. The Dutch mapmaker and astronomer Petrus Plancius took the notes Keyser and De Houtman had given him in 1595 and created new star maps of the skies. The Polish astronomers Johannes and Elisabeth Hevelius — Elisabeth is considered to be one of the first female astronomers — mapped stars from their own observatory and published charts of the new constellations such as Lynx and Leo Minor in the late 1600s.

APUS

LOCATION: SOUTHERN HEMISPHERE

Apus is a small constellation whose stars make a line with a narrow V on the end, much like the point of a beak.

HOW TO FIND IT

Apus is best seen between late July and Sept. in the southern **hemisphere** and in the area just north of the **equator**.

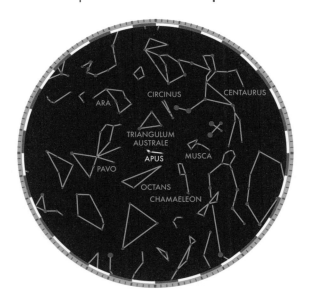

STORIES AND MYTHS

Hundreds of years ago, navigators from Europe traveled to the southern hemisphere and saw a beautiful bird they had never seen before, with striking colors and bright feathers: a bird of paradise. Initially they thought the bird was footless and marveled at such a strange creature, but it turns out they were mistaken — the bird was not footless after all! The navigators named this star group after that bird, calling it Apus, which reminds us of this mix-up, as the word comes from the Greek word *apous*, meaning "footless."

THE BIRD OF PARADISE

☀ **ALPHA APODIS**

Alpha Apodis is the brightest
star in Apus.

CAMELOPARDALIS

Camelopardalis is a large constellation with faint stars that can best be seen in a very dark sky. Its stars make a shape that looks like a giraffe.

HOW TO FIND IT

Camelopardalis is best seen between late Dec. and March in the northern **hemisphere** and just south of the **equator**.

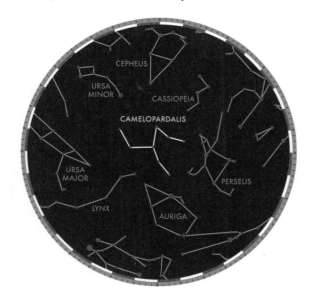

STORIES AND MYTHS

Camelopardalis is a Greek name that means "camel leopard," for an animal with a long neck like a camel and a body that is covered in "spots" — otherwise known as a giraffe! This constellation was named by the Dutch astronomer Petrus Plancius in the 1600s based on information he received from Dutch **navigators**.

THE GIRAFFE

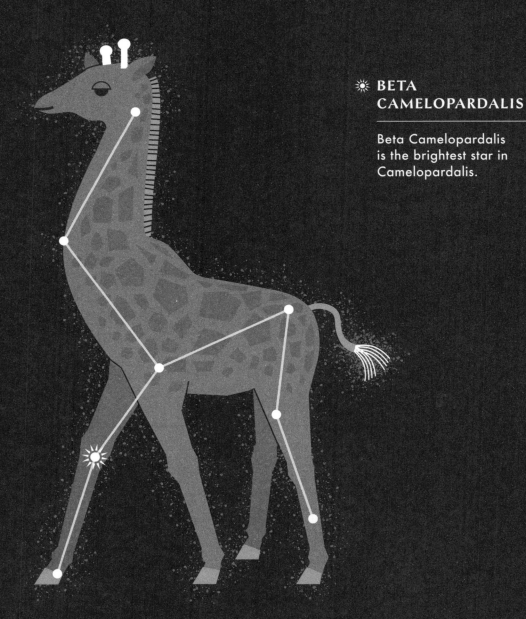

☀ **BETA CAMELOPARDALIS**

Beta Camelopardalis is the brightest star in Camelopardalis.

CANES VENATICI

LOCATION: NORTHERN HEMISPHERE

Canes Venatici is a medium-sized constellation that forms a very simple line.

HOW TO FIND IT

Canes Venatici is best seen between late March and June from anywhere except for the bottom half of the southern **hemisphere**.

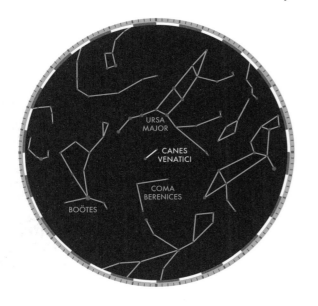

STORIES AND MYTHS

The two hunting dogs — Canes Venatici in Latin — are held on two leads by Boötes the Herdsman, who follows Ursa Major and Ursa Minor. The dogs did not exist as a constellation in ancient times, but were added to Boötes's hands much later in an area of the sky that the ancient Greeks could not see very well and presumed it had no stars. The dogs are named Chara, which is the Greek for "joy," and Asterion, which is the Greek for "little star."

THE HUNTING DOGS

☀ COR CAROLI

Cor Caroli (Alpha Canum Venaticorum) is the brightest star in Canes Venatici and means "Charles's heart" in Latin. It was named after King Charles I of England.

CHAMAELEON

LOCATION: SOUTHERN HEMISPHERE

Chamaeleon is a small constellation whose stars make up a shape that looks like a frying pan! In fact, that is what many people in Australia call it. The Chamaeleon's diamond shape and straight line can be hard to spot in the sky — just like a real chameleon!

HOW TO FIND IT

Chamaeleon is best seen between late March and June in the southern **hemisphere**.

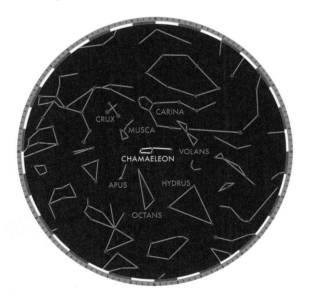

STORIES AND MYTHS

A chameleon is an amazing type of lizard that can change the appearance of its skin to blend in with its surroundings in order to hide from predators. The Dutch explorers who created this constellation probably saw many chameleons in Madagascar, which was one of the interesting stops they made on their journey through the southern hemisphere to chart the stars.

THE CHAMELEON

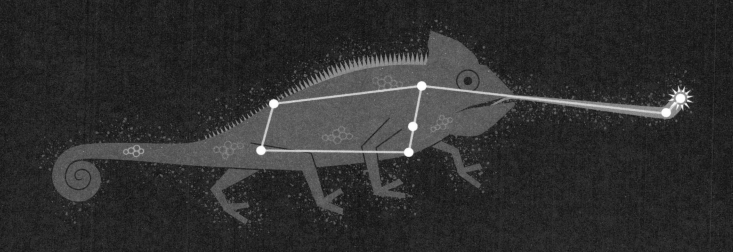

☀ **ALPHA CHAMAELEONTIS**

Alpha Chamaeleontis is the brightest star in Chamaeleon.

COLUMBA

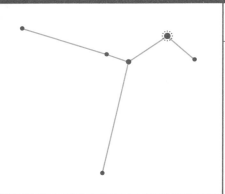

Columba is a small but bright constellation that looks like two V shapes stuck together. It sits near a big dog (Canis Major) and a rabbit (Lepus) in the sky, which might make some doves nervous!

HOW TO FIND IT

It is best seen between late Dec. and March in the southern **hemisphere** and in the lower half of the northern hemisphere.

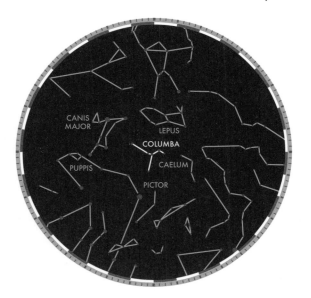

STORIES AND MYTHS

Columba is the Latin word for "dove," a beautiful white bird that is similar to a pigeon, but smaller. One story is that this dove is the bird from Noah's Ark in the Bible. After 40 days on the water following a worldwide flood, Noah sent out the bird to see if the waters were drying up. The dove came back with an olive branch in its beak, which proved to Noah that there was dry land nearby. In Greek mythology, a dove was sent out by the Argonauts on their journey to find the Golden Fleece to make sure they could pass through a pair of deadly clashing rocks. When the dove made it through, the Argonauts knew they could, too. Doves are known for being peaceful creatures that bring good news.

THE DOVE

☀ **PHACT**

Phact (Alpha Columbae) is the brightest star in Columba, and is based on an Arabic word that means "ring dove."

DORADO

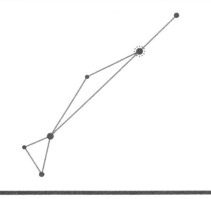

LOCATION: SOUTHERN HEMISPHERE

Dorado is a very small constellation which is located near the **Large Magellanic Cloud**. Its stars make up two triangle shapes connected to a straight line. It actually looks a lot like a swordfish and is sometimes pictured as one!

HOW TO FIND IT

Dorado is best seen between late Dec. and March from the southern **hemisphere** and southern parts of the northern hemisphere.

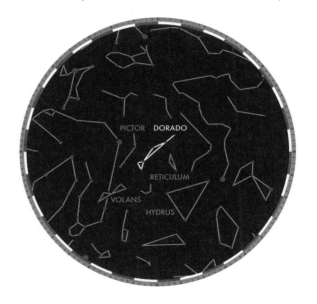

STORIES AND MYTHS

Dorado means "golden" or "dolphinfish" in Spanish. Dolphinfish are found in warm tropical waters and are not related to dolphins; they are much smaller and look completely different. Dolphinfish are called "mahimahi" in Pacific waters. Dutch explorers were so excited about all of the amazing creatures they saw on their travels in the southern hemisphere that they created many constellations in honor of them. They had seen dolphinfish chasing flying fish, so they placed the constellation Dorado next to Volans (the Flying Fish).

THE DOLPHINFISH

 **ALPHA DORADUS**

Alpha Doradus is the
brightest star in Dorado.

GRUS

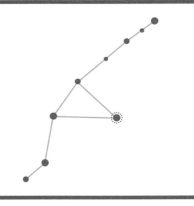

Grus is a medium-sized constellation whose stars form a curved line with a triangle coming off one side.

HOW TO FIND IT

Grus is best seen between late Sept. and Dec. from the southern **hemisphere** and the bottom third of the northern hemisphere.

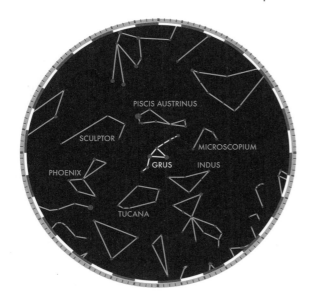

PISCIS AUSTRINUS

SCULPTOR

MICROSCOPIUM

GRUS

INDUS

PHOENIX

TUCANA

STORIES AND MYTHS

The crane, *grus* in Latin, is a tall, elegant bird. In the late 1500s, the Dutch astronomer Petrus Plancius asked two Dutch **navigators** sailing to the Indian Ocean to map constellations in the southern sky. With their information, Plancius created 12 new constellations and named them after newly discovered exotic animals. Grus has also been pictured as a heron or a flamingo. Plancius "took" some of its stars from another constellation: they used to be part of the Southern Fish (Piscis Austrinus), which is why some of its stars' names refer to fish!

THE CRANE

Alnair (Alpha Gruis) is the brightest star in Grus, and its name comes from an Arabic phrase meaning the "bright one."

HYDRUS

Hydrus is a small and simple constellation whose stars make a triangular shape.

HOW TO FIND IT

Hydrus is best seen from late Sept. to Dec. from the southern **hemisphere** and the area just above the **equator**.

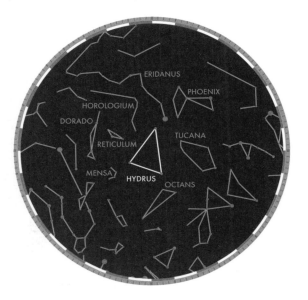

STORIES AND MYTHS

The lesser water snake, *hydrus* in Latin, should not be confused with the other water snake constellation, Hydra. Hydrus was named by astronomer Petrus Plancius, most likely after the sea snakes that were observed by Dutch **navigators** in the southern seas.

THE LESSER WATER SNAKE

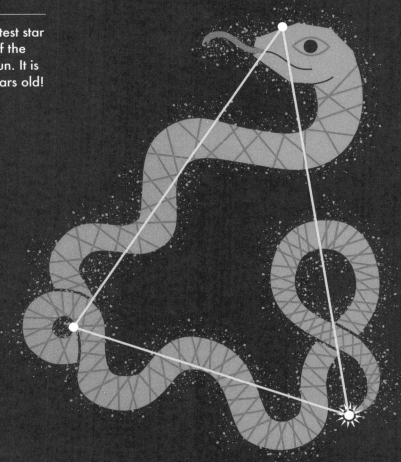

☀ **BETA HYDRI**

Beta Hydri is the brightest star in Hydrus and is one of the oldest stars near the Sun. It is almost seven billion years old!

INDUS

Indus is a smaller constellation whose stars make an irregular triangular shape.

HOW TO FIND IT

Indus is best seen between late June and Sept. from the southern **hemisphere** and the far south of the northern hemisphere.

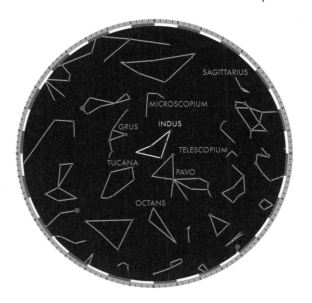

STORIES AND MYTHS

This constellation was originally pictured as an indigenous person who the Dutch explorers met on their travels in the East Indies, southern Africa, or Madagascar hundreds of years ago. The use of the term "Indian" (*indus* in Latin) to refer to any indigenous person shows us how the explorers wrongly thought that indigenous people were all the same rather than being individuals with specific names for their tribes or nations. Rather than seeing a version of that image here, why don't you imagine what picture this constellation could become?

THE INDIAN

☀ **ALPHA INDI**

Alpha Indi is the brightest
star in Indus, a constellation
with very few bright stars.

LACERTA

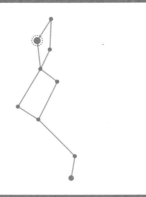

LOCATION: NORTHERN HEMISPHERE

Lacerta is a small constellation whose stars make an overall W shape like the shape of Cassiopeia, but smaller. It is sometimes even called "Little Cassiopeia." When the fainter stars are included in its shape, it resembles two connected diamonds.

HOW TO FIND IT

Lacerta is best seen between late Sept. and Dec. from anywhere except the lower half of the southern **hemisphere**.

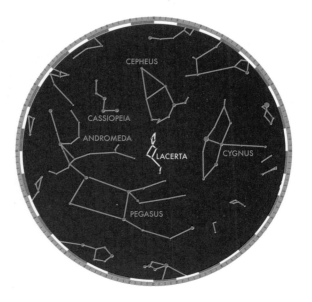

STORIES AND MYTHS

Lacerta, which is Latin for "lizard," is a small constellation that was originally called Stellio, after a type of lizard called a stellion, or starred agama, which has a star like pattern on it and is found in the Mediterranean. Lacerta was named by Polish astronomers Elisabeth and Johannes Hevelius, who used animals to identify many of the constellations they mapped. Later, it was generalized to be simply The Lizard.

THE LIZARD

☀ **ALPHA LACERTAE**

Alpha Lacertae is the
brightest star in Lacerta.

LEO MINOR

Leo Minor is one of the smallest constellations in the sky, and its stars make a diamond shape with a line coming off one side, like a kite flying sideways.

HOW TO FIND IT

Leo Minor is best seen between late March and June from anywhere except the lower half of the southern **hemisphere**.

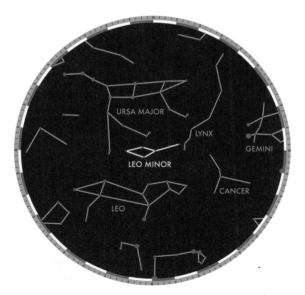

STORIES AND MYTHS

Leo Minor, which means the "little lion" in Latin, is a baby lion, or "cub," that was added above the much larger Leo constellation by astronomers Elisabeth and Johannes Hevelius in the 1600s to fill in a dark place in the sky. There are no myths or stories yet for Leo Minor — maybe you can think of one?

THE LITTLE LION

☀ **PRAECIPUA**

Praecipua (46 Leonis Minoris) is the brightest star in Leo Minor and has an orange color when you look at it through binoculars. Its name means "chief."

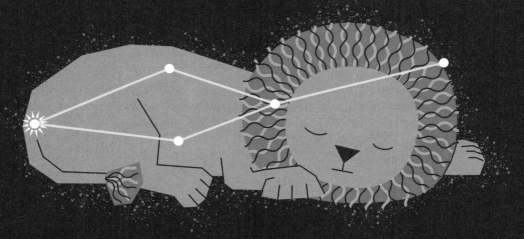

LYNX

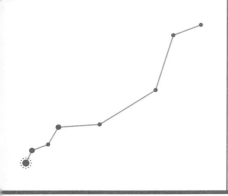

LOCATION: NORTHERN HEMISPHERE

Lynx is a medium-sized constellation that is hard to find because its stars are so faint, but its stars make a long, zigzag line.

HOW TO FIND IT

Lynx is best seen from March to June from anywhere except the lower half of the southern **hemisphere**.

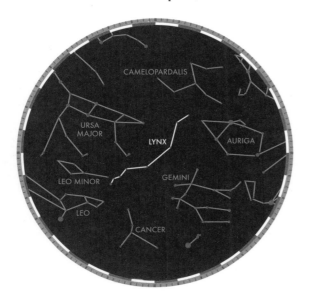

STORIES AND MYTHS

A lynx is a type of wild cat admired for its amazing eyesight and ability to spot prey from very far away. So when Polish astronomer Johannes Hevelius linked a group of faint stars in an open area of the sky between other constellations, he named it Lynx, because he said it would take the eyesight of a lynx to be able to observe such hard-to-see stars.

THE LYNX

☀ **ALPHA LYNCIS**

Alpha Lyncis is the brightest
star in Lynx.

MONOCEROS

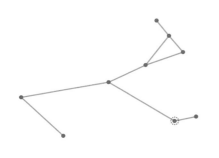

LOCATION: EQUATORIAL

Monoceros is a medium-sized constellation whose stars make the shape of a sitting animal with a triangle-shaped head and a single horn.

HOW TO FIND IT

Monoceros is best seen between late Dec. and March from nearly everywhere on Earth where people live.

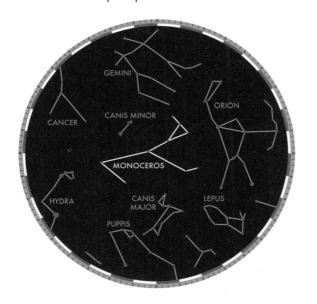

STORIES AND MYTHS

Today we know that unicorns don't exist, because nobody has ever seen one, but in the early 1600s, the time this constellation was named by Petrus Plancius, unicorns — mythical horse like creatures with a magical single horn — were thought to be real. They were known as a symbol of purity and gentleness, and it was said that a unicorn could make river water pure and safe to drink with the touch of its magical horn.

THE UNICORN

☀ **BETA MONOCEROTIS**

Beta Monocerotis is the
brightest star in Monoceros.

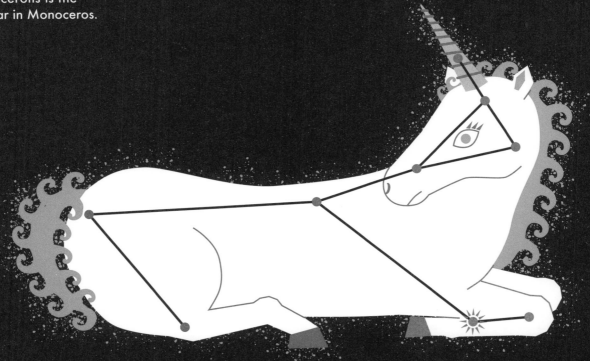

MUSCA

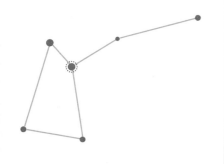

LOCATION: SOUTHERN HEMISPHERE

Musca is a very small constellation near the constellation Crux. Its stars make a shape that slightly resembles the Big Dipper, but really looks more like a pointy spoon.

HOW TO FIND IT

Musca is best seen between late March and June from the southern **hemisphere** and the area just above the **equator**.

STORIES AND MYTHS

The word for fly in Latin is *musca*, which sounds like and is related to the word "mosquito." This constellation was originally named after one of the insects Dutch explorers encountered in their travels in the southern hemisphere many hundreds of years ago. It is the only insect constellation in the sky. Some old illustrations show the nearby constellation, Chamaeleon, trying (but not succeeding) to eat Musca as a snack.

THE MODERN CONSTELLATIONS · ANIMALS AND PEOPLE

THE FLY

☀ **ALPHA MUSCAE**

Alpha Muscae is the brightest
star in Musca.

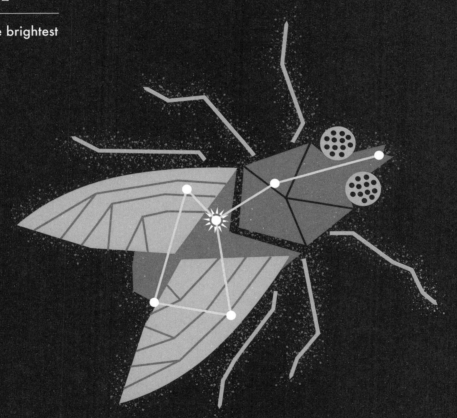

PAVO

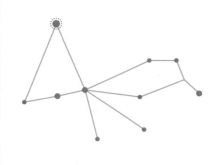

Pavo is a medium-sized constellation whose stars form a bird- or fish like-shape.

HOW TO FIND IT

Pavo is best seen between late June and Sept. from the southern **hemisphere** and the bottom third of the northern hemisphere.

STORIES AND MYTHS

Can you imagine seeing a peacock pulling a chariot through the sky? That was how the Greek queen of the gods, Hera, traveled around the earth and in the sky in ancient times. Although Pavo, which means "peacock" in Latin, was one of the southern birds that Dutch explorers added to the constellations in modern times, it has an important place in ancient Greek myths as Hera's sacred bird.

THE PEACOCK

Peacock (Alpha Pavonis) is Pavo's brightest star. It was given a name in English just before World War II, when the British Royal Air Force asked that all stars used for navigation be given names that were easier to remember.

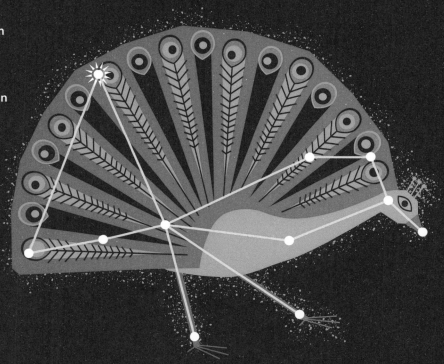

PHOENIX

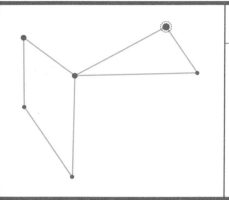

Phoenix is a medium-sized constellation whose stars form the shape of a diamond and a triangle stuck together.

HOW TO FIND IT

Phoenix is best seen between late Sept. and Dec. from the southern **hemisphere** and the bottom third of the northern hemisphere.

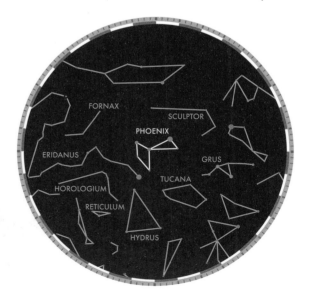

STORIES AND MYTHS

The phoenix was thought to be a very large, beautiful, and brightly colored mythical bird that could live forever. Some stories say that it dies in a burst of fire and is then reborn from the ashes of that fire. It is also associated with the Sun rising and setting. In many cultures, the phoenix represents the idea of death and rebirth, or making a "comeback." The Phoenix is one of the 12 constellations named after exotic or mythical creatures by the Dutch **navigators**.

THE PHOENIX

☀ **ANKAA**

Ankaa (Alpha Phoenicis) comes from an Arabic word for "phoenix" and is the brightest star in this constellation.

TUCANA

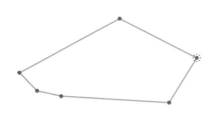

LOCATION: SOUTHERN HEMISPHERE

Tucana is a medium-sized constellation with faint stars that make an irregular **polygon** shape.

HOW TO FIND IT

Tucana is best seen between late Sept. and Dec. from the southern **hemisphere** and the bottom quarter of the northern hemisphere.

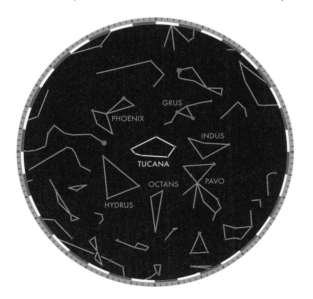

STORIES AND MYTHS

The Toucan — *tucana* in Latin — is part of a constellation group called the "celestial" or "southern birds," which includes Apus, Grus, Pavo, and Phoenix. Toucans are native to the rainforests and jungles of Central and South America and would have been seen by the Dutch **navigators** who helped chart the southern sky. You can recognize a toucan by its beak, because it is unusually large and often very colorful.

THE TOUCAN

☀ **ALPHA TUCANAE**

Alpha Tucanae is the
brightest star in Tucana.

VOLANS

Volans is a very small constellation whose stars make two connected side-by-side triangles.

HOW TO FIND IT

Volans is best seen between late Dec. and March from the southern **hemisphere** and the area just above the **equator**.

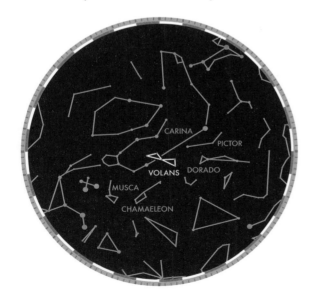

STORIES AND MYTHS

Have you ever seen a flying fish? A flying fish is a type of tropical fish that can jump very high out of the water, and then use its wing like fins to glide through the air. Dutch **navigators** who saw flying fish in their travels named this constellation in their honor. Volans, which is Latin for "flying," is usually pictured being chased by the dolphinfish of the constellation Dorado, which is what happens with flying fish and dolphinfish in real life!

THE FLYING FISH

☀ **BETA VOLANTIS**

Beta Volantis is the brightest
star in Volans.

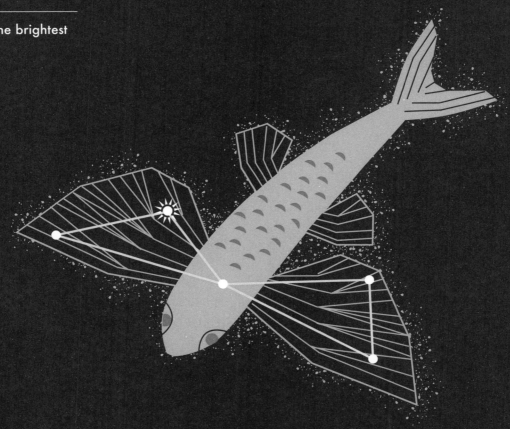

VULPECULA

LOCATION: NORTHERN HEMISPHERE

Vulpecula is a small constellation whose stars form a simple, straight line.

HOW TO FIND IT

Vulpecula is best seen between late June and Sept. from anywhere except the southernmost parts of the southern **hemisphere**.

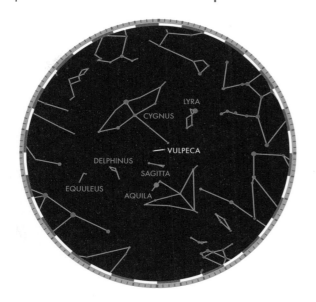

STORIES AND MYTHS

Originally, Polish astronomer Johannes Hevelius pictured this constellation as a duo: a fox returning from the hunt holding a goose in his mouth. He placed it near two other hunting animals: Aquila the eagle, and a vulture image that was an ancient interpretation of Lyra, the lyre constellation. Then he divided it into two distinct animals: *anser*, which is Latin for "goose," and *vulpecula*, which means "little fox." Today, the goose is no longer in the picture (perhaps it was eaten by the fox!), but it is remembered in the name of Vulpecula's brightest star, Anser.

☀ **ANSER**

Anser (Alpha Vulpecula)
comes from the Latin word
for "goose" and is the
brightest star in Vulpecula.

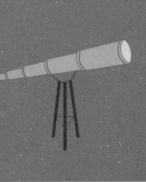

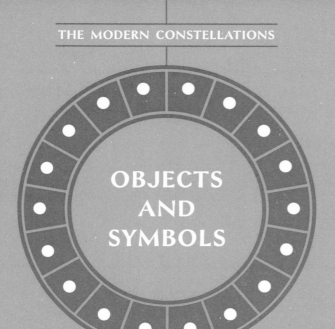

OBJECTS AND SYMBOLS

For some, the idea of objects and tools as constellations might seem quite dull compared to mythological characters and their exciting stories. But the French astronomer Nicolas Louis de Lacaille would disagree! In 1854, Lacaille traveled to the Cape of Good Hope in South Africa and spent two years cataloging more than 10,000 stars in the southern skies and created 14 new constellations, including Mensa, in honor of South Africa's Table Mountain, which he could see from his observatory.

For explorers and astronomers such as Lacaille, the new scientific tools were incredibly important because they allowed people to do and see things they never dreamed could be possible. For example, the microscope allowed scientists to look deep inside our everyday world, to see tiny particles and the way they fit together. The telescope gave the closest view yet of the stars and helped astronomers to better understand the universe and our place in it. And they didn't forget the artists and the tools they used to draw these new images seen in the sky.

ANTLIA

Antlia is a small constellation whose stars make an upside-down V shape.

HOW TO FIND IT

Antlia is best seen between late March and June from anywhere except for the top half of the northern **hemisphere**.

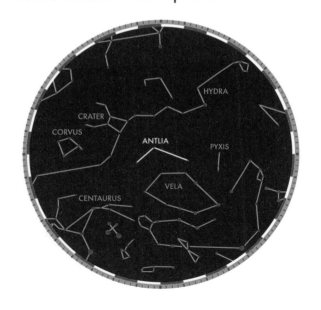

STORIES AND MYTHS

An air pump is a device that pushes air through an object or mechanism for various purposes — it's still used today to fix flat bicycle tyres or to aerate or pump aquariums with the oxygen that fish need to live and grow. Antlia, originally named Antlia Pneumatica, was created by French astronomer Nicolas Louis de Lacaille, who worked at a time when the world was looking to new possibilities in **engineering** and **physics**. Antlia was created as a symbol of and tribute to new inventions and innovations.

THE AIR PUMP

☀ **ALPHA ANTLIAE**

Alpha Antliae is the brightest
star in Antlia.

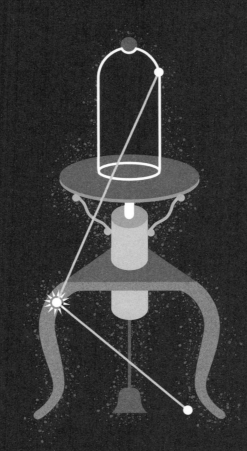

CAELUM

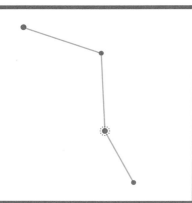

Caelum is one of the smallest constellations in the sky. Its stars make a simple shape that looks a bit like a hook.

HOW TO FIND IT

Caelum is best seen between late Dec. and March from anywhere except for the top half of the northern **hemisphere.**

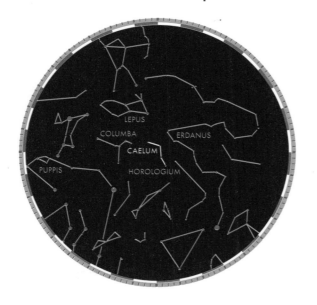

STORIES AND MYTHS

Caelum was originally called Caelum Scalptoris by Nicolas Louis de Lacaille, after a sculptor or engraver's chisel, a tool that was invented in the seventeenth century when book printing became popular. This particular chisel might have been used to carve fine lines into printing plates so that artistic imagery of the constellations and other subjects could be reproduced many times to be included in books. Its name was later simplified to Caelum.

THE CHISEL

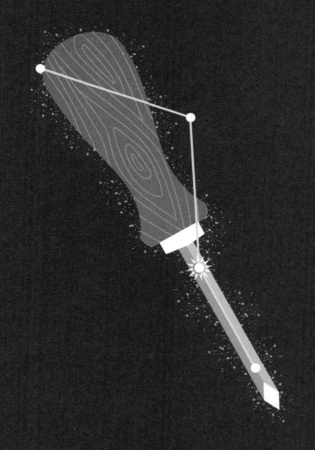

☀ **ALPHA CAELI**

Alpha Caeli is the constellation's brightest star. It is actually a binary **star system**, which is made up of two stars that circle each other.

CIRCINUS

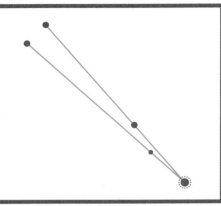

Circinus is the fourth-smallest constellation in the sky. It forms a narrow V shape.

HOW TO FIND IT

Circinus is best seen between late June and Sept. from the southern **hemisphere** and the lower third of the northern hemisphere.

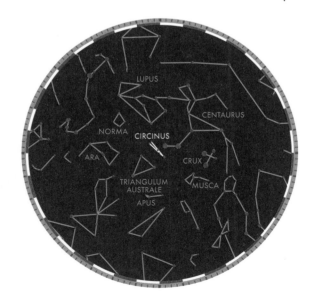

STORIES AND MYTHS

Have you ever wondered how to draw a perfect circle? Circinus is the Latin word for "a pair of compasses," which is a tool that helps people such as engineers and designers draw perfectly round circles. The astronomer Nicolas Louis de Lacaille, who named Circinus, spent two years at the southern tip of South Africa mapping more than 10,000 stars in the sky. He also created 14 new constellations and named them after tools that were important to scientists and inventors.

THE COMPASSES

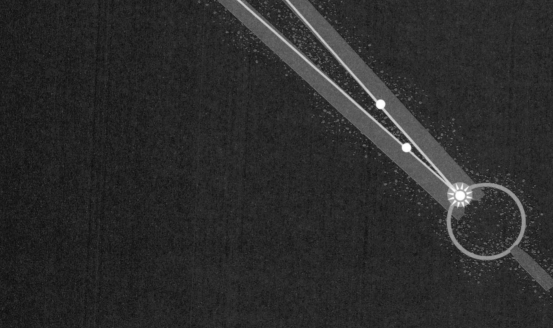

☀ **ALPHA CIRCINI**

Alpha Circini is the brightest
star in Circinus.

CRUX

LOCATION: SOUTHERN HEMISPHERE

Crux, the smallest constellation in the sky, sits in the Milky Way and its stars form a cross shape. It's also known as an **asterism** called the Southern Cross. Crux has been an important tool for navigation, because it has very bright stars and it points to the **south celestial pole**.

HOW TO FIND IT

Crux is best seen between late March and June from the southern **hemisphere** and the southern parts of the northern hemisphere.

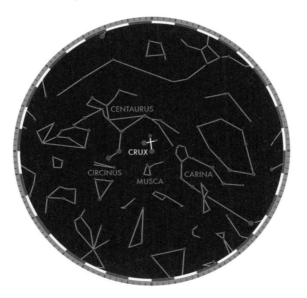

STORIES AND MYTHS

The name Crux comes from the Latin word for "cross." Originally, around 2,000 years ago, the stars of this constellation were considered to be part of Centaurus's back leg, but because the tilt of Earth changed over time, people in Europe could no longer see these stars and they were forgotten. When European explorers traveled to the southern hemisphere 500 years ago on their voyages of exploration, they rediscovered the stars and were struck by their resemblance to a Christian cross. They saw it as a good omen for their expeditions and for their mission to spread Christianity.

THE SOUTHERN CROSS

MIMOSA

Mimosa (Beta Crucis) is a first magnitude star, the 19th brightest in the sky, and the second-brightest star in Crux. A representation of the constellation Crux can be found on the national flags of Australia, Brazil, New Zealand, Papua New Guinea, and Samoa.

ACRUX

Acrux (Alpha Crucis) is also a first magnitude star, the 13th brightest in the sky and the brightest star in Crux. Its name comes from the **Bayer Designation** — a system of naming stars with Greek letters based on their brightness, created by German astronomer Johann Bayer. The "a" in Acrux comes from the word "alpha," which is the first letter of the Greek alphabet.

FORNAX

Fornax is a medium-sized constellation whose stars form a wide V shape.

HOW TO FIND IT

Fornax is best seen between late Dec. and March from the southern **hemisphere** and the lower half of the northern hemisphere.

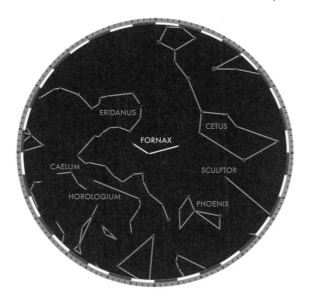

STORIES AND MYTHS

A furnace is a machine that creates high heat, a bit like a very complicated fireplace. Furnaces like the one illustrated in Fornax — named by Nicolas Louis de Lacaille and which is Greek for "oven" — were, and still are, used by scientists. The furnace pictured in the constellation was one used by chemists to separate liquids into their individual elements, such as minerals or other solids, or to remove harmful things such as bacteria. A modern-day version of a furnace is used to create decaffeinated coffee by separating out the caffeine particles!

THE FURNACE

HOROLOGIUM

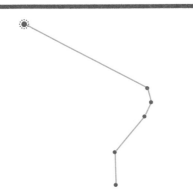

Horologium is one of the smaller constellations whose stars make up a long straight line that changes into a curved line at one end.

HOW TO FIND IT

Horologium is best seen between late Dec. and March from the southern **hemisphere** and the bottom third of the northern hemisphere.

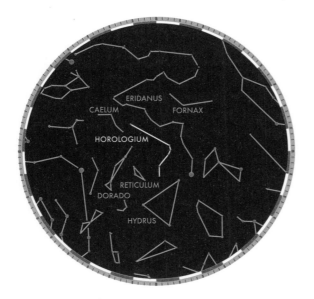

STORIES AND MYTHS

When this constellation was created and named in the 1700s by astronomer Nicolas Louis de Lacaille, there were no phones or digital devices, and the pendulum clock — *horologium* in Latin — was the most accurate way to keep time. A pendulum clock uses a swinging weight, called a pendulum, to count the seconds. Early pendulum clocks had this weight on the outside, but in time, the pendulum was encased for a shorter swing, like in a grandfather clock. Pendulum clocks helped early astronomers keep track of the position of the stars.

THE PENDULUM CLOCK

☀ **ALPHA HOROLOGII**

Alpha Horologii is the
brightest star in Horologium
and is often pictured as the
clock's pendulum.

MENSA

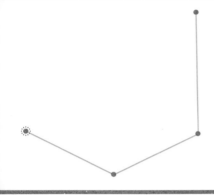

Mensa is a very small, hard-to-see constellation whose stars make a dome or bucket shape, depending on when you are looking at it.

HOW TO FIND IT

Mensa is best seen between late Dec. and March from the southern **hemisphere** and near the **equator** in the northern hemisphere.

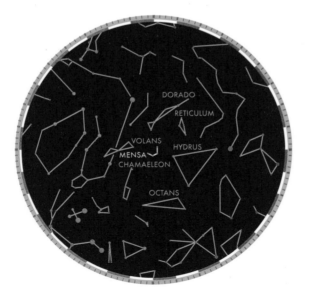

STORIES AND MYTHS

The Table Mountain — *mensa* in Latin — is a famous mountain that overlooks Cape Town in South Africa. It has a long, flat top, like a table. The French astronomer Nicolas Louis de Lacaille wanted to identify a constellation to honor the place where he had spent so much time cataloguing the southern stars. Sitting above the constellation Mensa is the misty **Large Magellanic Cloud**, which resembles the clouds that often cover the earthly Table Mountain.

THE TABLE MOUNTAIN

☀ **ALPHA MENSAE**

Alpha Mensae is the brightest
star in Mensa.

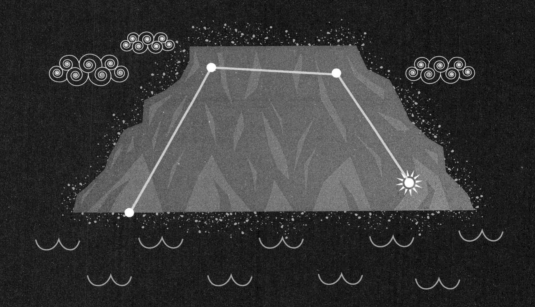

MICROSCOPIUM

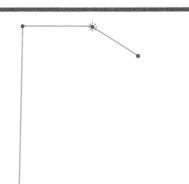

Microscopium is a very small, faint constellation whose stars make a shape like a lower case *r*.

HOW TO FIND IT

Microscopium is best seen from late June through Sept. from anywhere except the top half of the northern **hemisphere**.

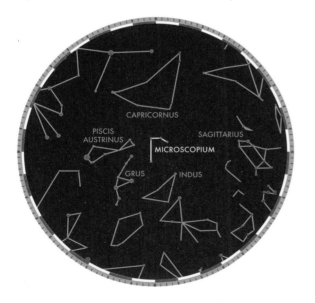

STORIES AND MYTHS

A microscope is a tool that uses a lens to make tiny things look larger. It is one of the many scientific tools that were new and exciting at the time this constellation was introduced. The microscope in this illustration is a modern version that is more like what you might see today. The astronomer who named it, Nicolas Louis de Lacaille, borrowed a few stars from Sagittarius's hind legs to complete his picture.

THE MICROSCOPE

☀ GAMMA MICROSCOPII

Gamma Microscopii is the brightest star in Microscopium.

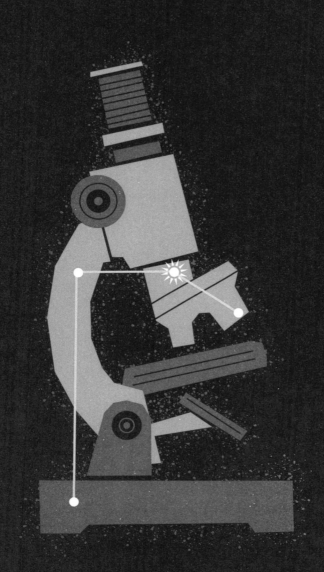

NORMA

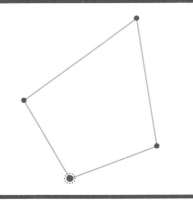

Norma is a very small constellation whose stars make the shape of an irregular **polygon**.

HOW TO FIND IT

Norma is best seen between late June and Sept. from the southern **hemisphere** and the bottom third of the northern hemisphere.

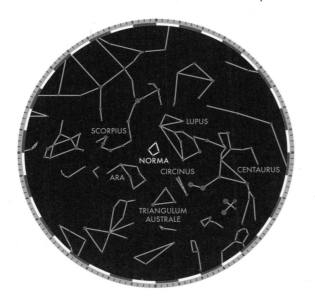

STORIES AND MYTHS

It's important that engineers, carpenters, and draughtspeople make accurate and detailed drawings of their plans for machines, inventions, or buildings. A set square — *norma* in Latin — is a tool that is used to draw perfect corners, also known as right angles. When this constellation was created hundreds of years ago by Nicolas Louis de Lacaille, it was a time of many exciting new inventions, so it was important to be able to make accurate drawings and plans for those ideas.

THE SET SQUARE

☀ **GAMMA² NORMAE**

Gamma² Normae is the brightest star in Norma.

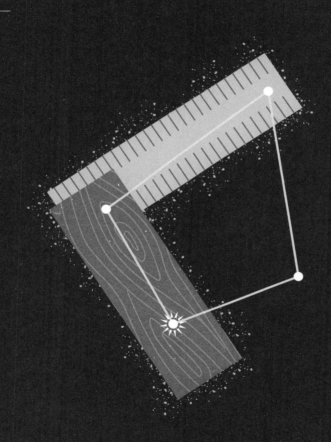

OCTANS

LOCATION: SOUTHERN HEMISPHERE

Octans is a medium-sized constellation whose stars make a thin triangle shape. It is home to the **south celestial pole**, an imaginary point in the sky above Earth's south pole.

HOW TO FIND IT

Octans is best seen between late Sept. and Dec. only from the southern **hemisphere**.

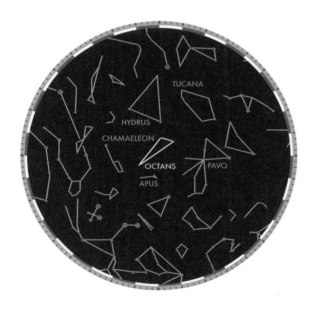

STORIES AND MYTHS

An octant is a tool that has been used for hundreds of years to help people navigate on the oceans by providing a very accurate way to view the stars. At the time this constellation was created by Nicolas Louis de Lacaille, the octant was a new invention and became a vital tool for sailors, **navigators**, and astronomers. An octant finds the angle between a star and the horizon, which tells the navigator how far north or south something is from Earth's **equator**. Octant comes from the Latin word for the "eighth part of a circle," which is the maximum angle it can measure.

THE OCTANT

☀ NU OCTANTIS

Nu Octantis is the brightest star in Octans.

✸ SIGMA OCTANTIS

Sigma Octantis is the southern pole star. It is the closest bright star to the south celestial pole.

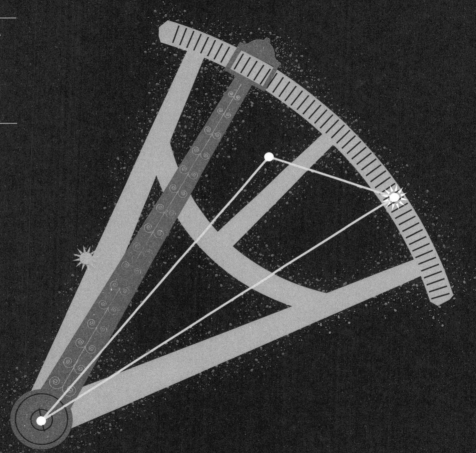

PICTOR

Pictor is a small constellation whose stars form a bent line shape. Most of its stars are faint, but because it sits near Canopus, the second-brightest star in the sky (found in the constellation Carina in Argo Navis), it is easy to find.

HOW TO FIND IT

Pictor is best seen between late Dec. and March from the southern **hemisphere** and the lower third of the northern hemisphere.

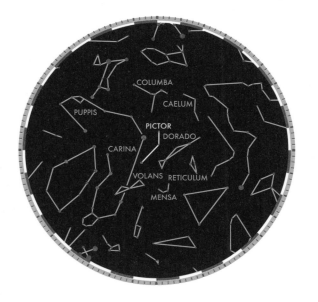

STORIES AND MYTHS

Before there were photographs and cameras, the only way to record the stars was to draw them. Artists worked hard to record exactly what they saw in the sky. Then other artists applied their imagination and skill to portray the mythological or scientific image associated with each constellation. It feels right to see artists honored with this constellation, which Nicolas Louis de Lacaille named after the Latin word for a painter's easel.

THE PAINTER'S EASEL

☀ **ALPHA PICTORIS**

Alpha Pictoris is Pictor's
brightest star.

PYXIS

Pyxis is a small constellation whose stars make a line of three stars.

HOW TO FIND IT

Pyxis is best seen between late March and June from the southern **hemisphere** and the lower half of the northern hemisphere.

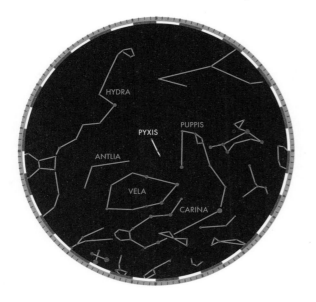

STORIES AND MYTHS

A nautical compass — *pyxis* in Latin — is a sailor's tool that looks a bit like an old-fashioned clock, but is used for navigation, not telling the time. It has a needle with a magnet in it. The magnet pulls the needle toward the north, so the person using it can always tell which direction they are facing. The compass was a vital tool, especially when the sky wasn't clear enough to navigate by the stars. The Pyxis constellation sits next to the Argo Navis in the sky, ready to be of use if any celestial Argonauts show up!

THE COMPASS

☀ ALPHA PYXIDIS

Alpha Pyxidis is the brightest star in Pyxis.

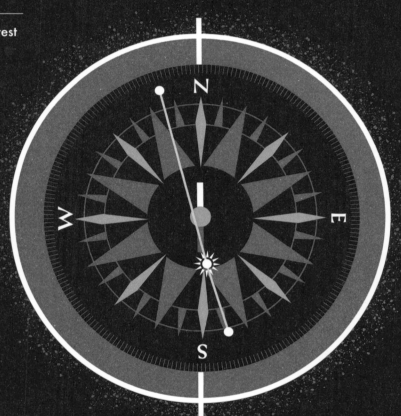

RETICULUM

Reticulum is one of the smallest constellations in the sky. Its stars make a tiny diamond shape.

HOW TO FIND IT

Reticulum is best seen between late Dec. and March from the southern **hemisphere** and the lower quarter of the northern hemisphere.

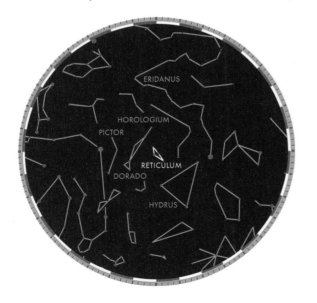

STORIES AND MYTHS

The small net — *reticulum* in Latin — pictured here is not a fishing net, but a tiny "net" of fine lines etched inside the lens of a telescope. These lines are used for looking at and measuring stars precisely. If you move a telescope so that a star is in the center of the net (or "reticle" in English), it can help you measure how big that star is and how far it is from other stars. Reticulum was originally called Rhombus by German astronomer Isaac Habrecht II because of its shape, but Nicolas Louis de Lacaille renamed it to honor a small but important element of the astronomer's telescope.

THE NET

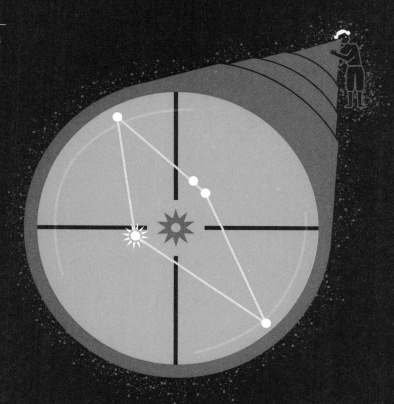

☀ **ALPHA RETICULI**

Alpha Reticuli is the brightest
star in Reticulum.

SCULPTOR

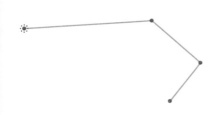

Sculptor is a medium-sized constellation with faint stars. Its stars make the shape of a hook.

HOW TO FIND IT

Sculptor is best seen between late Sept. and Dec. from anywhere except the top third of the northern **hemisphere**.

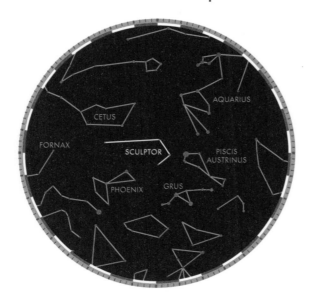

STORIES AND MYTHS

Although it was later shortened to simply Sculptor, this constellation was originally called *L'Atelier du Sculpteur*, French for "The Sculptor's Studio," which sounds like a very complicated scene based on such a simple shape! A carved bust (head-and-neck sculpture), and a three-legged table were imagined in this constellation by astronomer Nicolas Louis de Lacaille.

THE SCULPTOR

☀ ALPHA SCULPTORI

Alpha Sculptori is the brightest star in Sculptor.

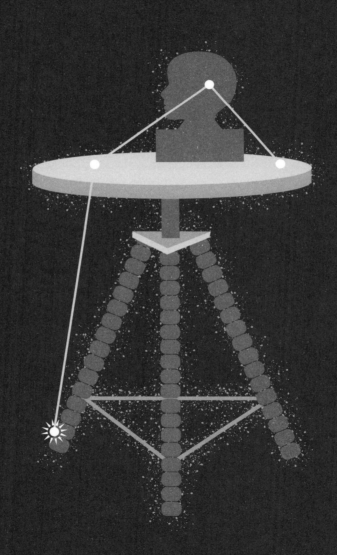

SCUTUM

Scutum is one of the smallest constellations. Its stars make up the shape of a long, narrow diamond.

HOW TO FIND IT

Scutum is best seen between late June and Sept. from nearly everywhere on Earth where people live.

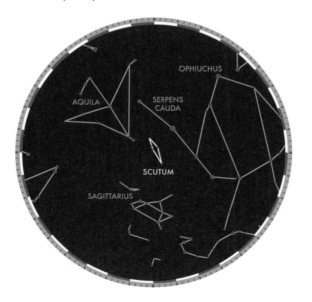

STORIES AND MYTHS

The original name for Scutum, which means "shield" in Latin, was Sobieski's Shield. It was named in honor of a Polish king who helped rebuild the astronomer Johannes Hevelius's **observatory** in 1679 after a terrible fire nearly destroyed it. Together with his wife, Elisabeth, Hevelius not only discovered constellations and produced the first atlas of the Moon, he also created and refined scientific instruments. The name of the constellation was later simplified to represent a plain shield. The "scutum" is a particular kind of shield that is oblong and curved.

THE SHIELD

☀ **ALPHA SCUTI**

Alpha Scuti is the brightest
star in Scutum.

SEXTANS

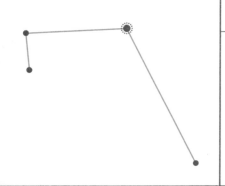

LOCATION: EQUATORIAL

Sextans is a medium-sized constellation with faint stars. Its stars make a hook shape.

HOW TO FIND IT

Sextans is best seen between late March and June from nearly everywhere on Earth where people live.

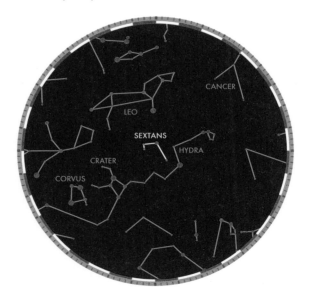

STORIES AND MYTHS

A sextant is a navigational tool like an octant, but instead of it being an eighth of a circle, its angle is a sixth of a circle. A sextant measures the angle between an object in the sky and the horizon and can help **navigators** determine **latitude** and **longitude**. The astronomer Johannes Hevelius's own treasured sextant, which was destroyed in a fire, was pictured in the first images of this constellation.

THE SEXTANT

☀ **ALPHA SEXTANTIS**

Alpha Sextantis is the
brightest star in Sextans.

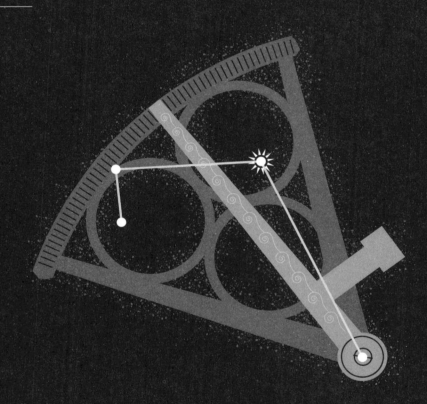

TELESCOPIUM

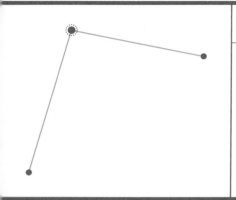

Telescopium is a small, faint constellation whose stars make a wide V shape.

HOW TO FIND IT

Telescopium is best seen between late June and Sept. from the southern **hemisphere** and the lower half of the northern hemisphere.

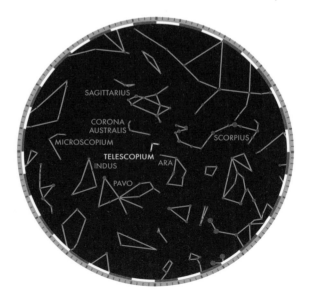

STORIES AND MYTHS

In a celestial space filled with other tool-inspired constellations, it makes perfect sense that Nicolas Louis de Lacaille included a telescope in his named constellations! A telescope is a tool that is used to make things that are far away appear closer. It has been a vital tool for astronomers to study the constellations. Now we have the ability to make powerful glass lenses, so our telescopes can be relatively short, but in earlier times telescopes had to be very long in order to work.

THE TELESCOPE

☀ **ALPHA TELESCOPII**

Alpha Telescopii is the
brightest star in Telescopium.

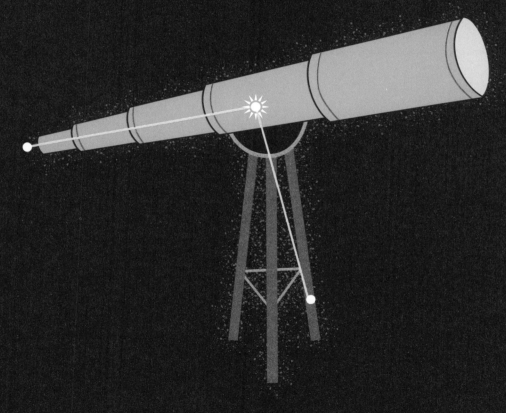

TRIANGULUM AUSTRALE

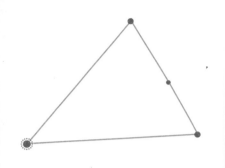

LOCATION: SOUTHERN HEMISPHERE

Triangulum Australe is one of the teeniest constellations in the sky. Its stars make a triangle shape that is even smaller than that of its northern counterpart, Triangulum.

HOW TO FIND IT

It is best seen between late June and Sept. from the southern **hemisphere** and the lower quarter of the northern hemisphere.

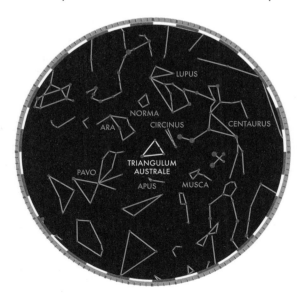

STORIES AND MYTHS

The Southern Triangle — Triangulum Australe in Latin — was recorded in a few different places in the sky before it landed where it is now. It was first imagined as a level by the Dutch astronomer Petrus Plancius, named after a scientific tool used to establish a perfectly horizontal plane, which is parallel to the horizon and helpful in measuring a star's distance. He called it Triangulum Antarcticus, but positioned it on a star globe in the wrong place. Astronomer Johann Bayer called it Triangulum Australe when he recorded it in his star charts and moved it to its correct position. Then Nicolas Louis de Lacaille renamed it to specifically represent a surveyor's level (*niveau*), *le Triangle Austral.*

THE SOUTHERN TRIANGLE

☀ **ATRIA**

Atria (Alpha Trianguli
Australis) is the brightest star
in Triangulum Australe and
is one of the brighter stars
in the southern sky.

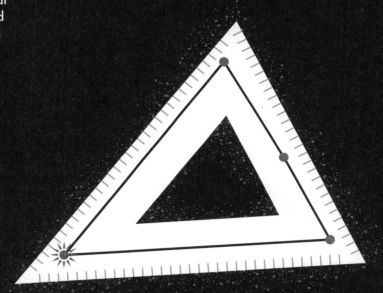

SKY MAPS
AND OTHER
RESOURCES

USEFUL TOOLS FOR STARGAZING

Here are a few excellent tools to help you further on your stargazing adventures!

PLANISPHERES
A planisphere is a circular star map that can be adjusted to show the location of the stars for specific times and locations. You can find them at some bookshops, science centers, and online retailers. You can also make your own with the help of an adult at in-the-sky.org/planisphere/index.php.

SMARTPHONE APPS
There are smartphone apps such as Skyview and Star Walk that allow you to point your phone at the sky to find out which stars or constellations you are looking at.

BOOKS
* *Find the Constellations* by H. A. Rey
* *The Stars* by H. A. Rey
* *Star Finder* by DK/Smithsonian

WEBSITES
With an adult's help you can visit these websites to see your current night view!
* theskylive.com/planetarium
* https://in-the-sky.org/skymap.php

HOW TO USE YOUR SKY MAPS

The sky maps on the following pages will help you find out where the constellations sit in relation to one another in the sky and how they would be oriented in the sky at particular dates and times of the year.

These maps show the entire night sky, but the area of the sky that you will see depends on where on Earth you are standing. For a more exact sky view on a precise date and time from your location, use a planisphere, an app, or a website.

When looking for the zodiac constellations on the maps, search along the dotted gold line that marks the **ecliptic** and you'll find them.

If you are located far to the north or far to the south, where the Sun shines until late at night, it will be tricky to see the constellations before it's time to go to bed, so you might have to do your skywatching during the winter when the Sun sets earlier.

✳ ✳ ✳

This is the approximate orientation and position of the constellations in relation to one another if you are facing south in the evening.

VIRGO

BOÖTES

SERPENS

COMA
BERENICES

LEO

CANES
VENATICI

CORONA
BOREALIS

HERCULES

LEO
MINOR

URSA
MAJOR

OPHIUCHUS

DRACO

HYDRA

URSA
MINOR

LYRA

CANCER

AQUILA

LYNX

CAMELOPARDALIS

CYGNUS

CANIS
MINOR

VULPECULA

GEMINI

SAGITTA

CEPHEUS

DELPHINUS

AURIGA

EQUULEUS

CASSIOPEIA

MILKY WAY

LACERTA

ORION

PERSEUS

ANDROMEDA

PEGASUS

TRIANGULUM

TAURUS

ARIES

THE ECLIPTIC

CETUS

PISCES

CONSTELLATIONS OF THE NORTHERN SKY FROM FEBRUARY TO APRIL

Remember, what stars you see in your sky will depend on where you are in the world. You may only see parts of these sky views. Use a planisphere, computer, or app for an exact sky view from your location.

This is the approximate orientation and position of the constellations in relation to one another if you are facing south in the evening.

AQUILA
OPHIUCHUS
SAGITTA
DELPHINUS
EQUULEUS
LYRA
VULPECULA
HERCULES
CYGNUS
PEGASUS
SERPENS
CORONA
BOREALIS
CEPHEUS
LACERTA
DRACO
ANDROMEDA
BOÖTES
PISCES
URSA
MINOR
CASSIOPEIA
TRIANGULUM
CANES
VENATICI
MILKY
WAY
COMA
BERENICES
ARIES
ARIES
VIRGO
CETUS
CAMELOPARDALIS
THE ECLIPTIC
URSA
MAJOR
PERSEUS
LEO
MINOR
LYNX
LEO
AURIGA
TAURUS
CANCER
ORION
GEMINI
HYDRA
CANIS
MINOR

199

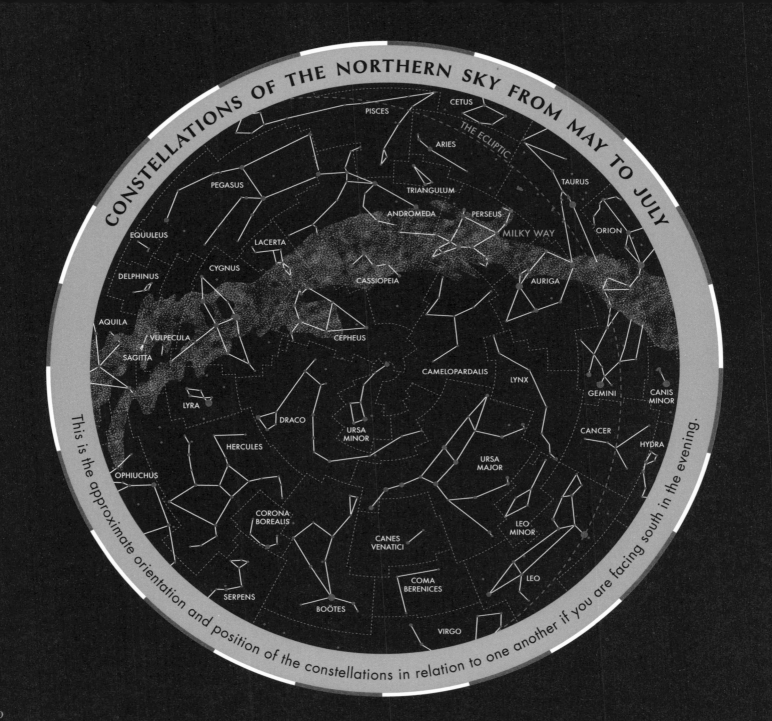

This is the approximate orientation and position of the constellations in relation to one another if you are facing south in the evening.

PISCES

CETUS

ARIES

THE ECLIPTIC

TRIANGULUM

TAURUS

PEGASUS

ANDROMEDA

PERSEUS

ORION

EQUULEUS

MILKY WAY

LACERTA

DELPHINUS

CYGNUS

CASSIOPEIA

AURIGA

AQUILA

CEPHEUS

VULPECULA

SAGITTA

CAMELOPARDALIS

LYNX

GEMINI

CANIS MINOR

LYRA

DRACO

URSA MINOR

CANCER

HYDRA

HERCULES

URSA MAJOR

OPHIUCHUS

LEO MINOR

CORONA BOREALIS

CANES VENATICI

LEO

SERPENS

COMA BERENICES

BOÖTES

VIRGO

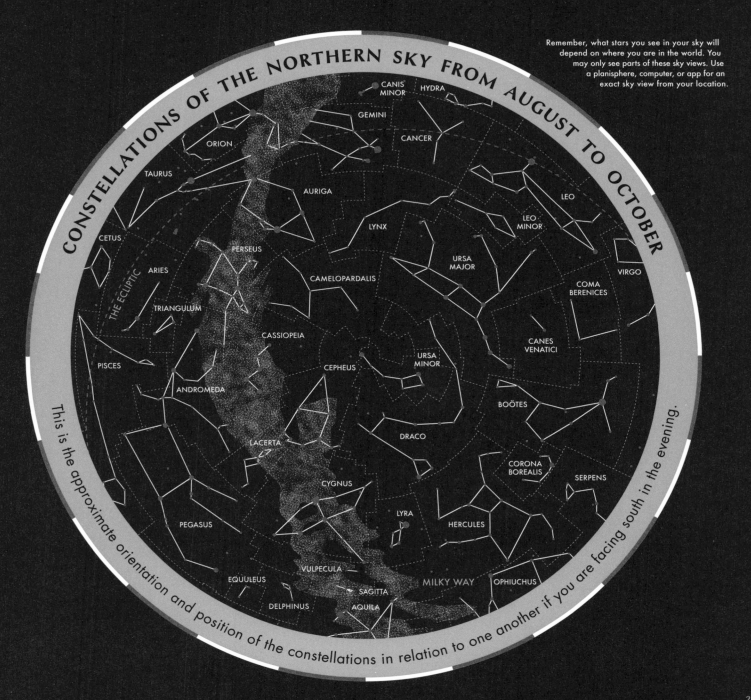

Remember, what stars you see in your sky will depend on where you are in the world. You may only see parts of these sky views. Use a planisphere, computer, or app for an exact sky view from your location.

This is the approximate orientation and position of the constellations in relation to one another if you are facing south in the evening.

CANIS MINOR
HYDRA
GEMINI
CANCER
ORION
TAURUS
AURIGA
LEO
LYNX
LEO MINOR
CETUS
PERSEUS
URSA MAJOR
VIRGO
ARIES
THE ECLIPTIC
CAMELOPARDALIS
COMA BERENICES
TRIANGULUM
CASSIOPEIA
CANES VENATICI
PISCES
URSA MINOR
CEPHEUS
ANDROMEDA
BOÖTES
DRACO
LACERTA
CORONA BOREALIS
SERPENS
CYGNUS
LYRA
PEGASUS
HERCULES
VULPECULA
MILKY WAY
OPHIUCHUS
EQUULEUS
SAGITTA
DELPHINUS
AQUILA

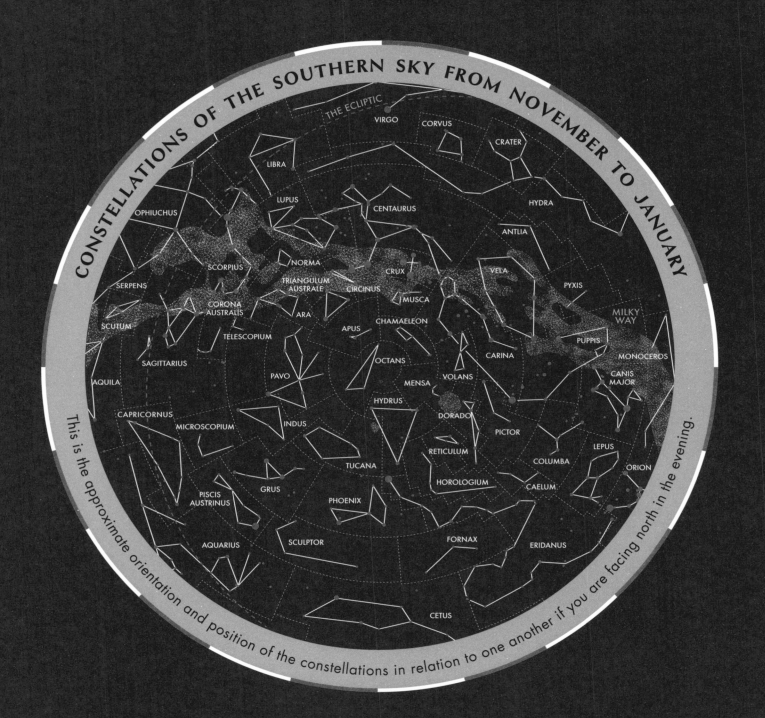

CONSTELLATIONS OF THE SOUTHERN SKY FROM FEBRUARY TO APRIL

Remember, what stars you see in your sky will depend on where you are in the world. You may only see parts of these sky views. Use a planisphere, computer, or app for an exact sky view from your location.

This is the approximate orientation and position of the constellations in relation to one another if you are facing north in the evening.

AQUILA
SCUTUM
SERPENS
CAPRICORNUS
SAGITTARIUS
OPHIUCHUS
MICROSCOPIUM
AQUARIUS
PISCIS AUSTRINUS
CORONA AUSTRALIS
SCORPIUS
LIBRA
INDUS
TELESCOPIUM
ARA
GRUS
PAVO
NORMA
LUPUS
PHOENIX
TRIANGULUM AUSTRALE
THE ECLIPTIC
SCULPTOR
TUCANA
OCTANS
APUS
CIRCINUS
VIRGO
CHAMAELEON
MUSCA
CRUX
CENTAURUS
HYDRUS
FORNAX
CETUS
HOROLOGIUM
MENSA
CORVUS
RETICULUM
VOLANS
DORADO
VELA
CRATER
PICTOR
CARINA
ANTLIA
CAELUM
ERIDANUS
PYXIS
HYDRA
COLUMBA
LEPUS
MILKY WAY
CANIS MAJOR
PUPPIS
ORION
MONOCEROS

203

Remember, what stars you see in your sky will depend on where you are in the world. You may only see parts of these sky views. Use a planisphere, computer, or app for an exact sky view from your location.

This is the approximate orientation and position of the constellations in relation to one another if you are facing north in the evening.

MONOCEROS
ORION
HYDRA
CANIS MAJOR
PUPPIS
LEPUS
PYXIS
COLUMBA
CAELUM
ERIDANUS
ANTLIA
PICTOR
CARINA
CRATER
VELA
CORVUS
VOLANS
MILKY WAY
DORADO
MENSA
RETICULUM
HOROLOGIUM
FORNAX
CETUS
CENTAURUS
VIRGO
HYDRUS
CRUX
MUSCA
CHAMAELEON
THE ECLIPTIC
CIRCINUS
TUCANA
SCULPTOR
APUS
OCTANS
PHOENIX
LUPUS
TRIANGULUM AUSTRALE
NORMA
PAVO
LIBRA
ARA
GRUS
INDUS
SCORPIUS
TELESCOPIUM
PISCIS AUSTRINUS
OPHIUCHUS
CORONA AUSTRALIS
MICROSCOPIUM
AQUARIUS
CAPRICORNUS
SAGITTARIUS
SERPENS
SCUTUM
AQUILA

205

MORE ABOUT ASTERISMS

Here is a list of well-known **asterisms** and the constellation area in which each one lives. **Asterisms** can be very helpful tools for finding constellations, as they often include very bright stars and have distinct shapes that are easy to spot. Not all **asterisms** are found within constellations. Some of them are shared by more than one constellation!

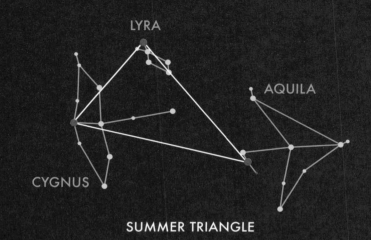

LYRA

AQUILA

CYGNUS

SUMMER TRIANGLE

SAGITTARIUS

TEAPOT

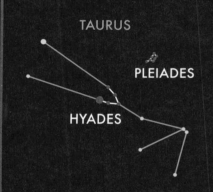

TAURUS

PLEIADES

HYADES

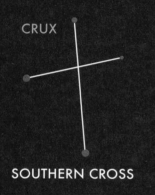

CRUX

SOUTHERN CROSS

URSA MINOR

LITTLE DIPPER

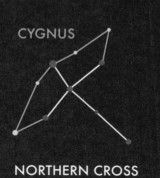

CYGNUS

NORTHERN CROSS

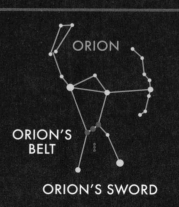

ORION

ORION'S BELT

ORION'S SWORD

URSA MAJOR

BIG DIPPER

DELPHINUS

JOB'S COFFIN

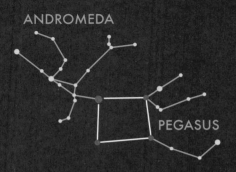

GREAT SQUARE OF PEGASUS

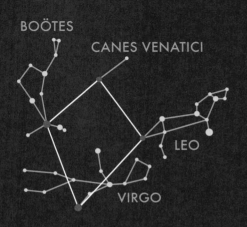

GREAT DIAMOND

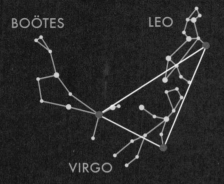

SPRING TRIANGLE

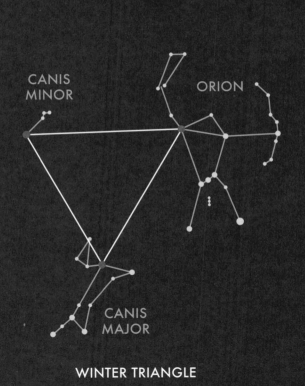

WINTER TRIANGLE

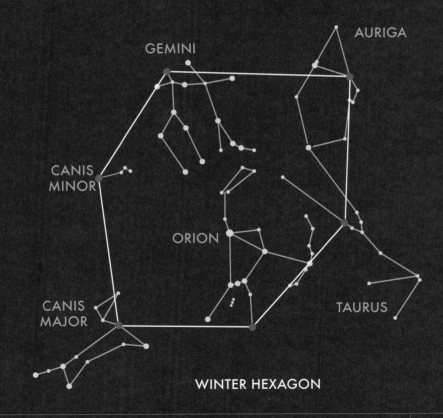

WINTER HEXAGON

MORE ABOUT ASTRONOMY

Do you want to learn more about the universe? Astronomers know all about stars, but they also know about black holes, gravity, the Sun, and loads of other things! To learn more about **astronomy**, visit your local library to check out these books, or with the help of an adult, visit these websites.

BOOKS
* *The Astronomy Book* by DK
* *Ultimate Explorer Field Guide: Night Sky: Find Adventure! Go Outside! Have Fun! Be a Backyard Stargazer! (National Geographic Kids Ultimate Explorer Field Guide)* by Howard Schneider
* *Scholastic Discover More: Night Sky* by Giles Sparrow
* *Space! (Knowledge Encyclopedias)* by DK

WEBSITES
* kidsastronomy.com
* almanac4kids.com/sky
* nasa.gov/kidsclub
* ducksters.com/science/astronomy.php

*   *   *

MORE ABOUT GREEK MYTHOLOGY

You have met some of the characters from ancient Greek mythology in this book, but there are so many more to discover! If you would like to learn more about Greek myths, visit your local library to check out these books, or with the help of an adult, visit these websites.

BOOKS
* *D'Aulaires' Book of Greek Myths* by Ingri and Edgar Parin D'Aulaire
* *Greek Myths* by Ann Turnbull
* *Mythology: Timeless Tales of Gods and Heroes* by Edith Hamilton

WEBSITES
* natgeokids.com/nz/discover/history/greece/greek-myths/#!/register
* greece.mrdonn.org/myths.html
* ducksters.com/history/ancient_greek_mythology.php
* historyforkids.net/ancient-greek-gods.html

*   *   *

MORE ABOUT CONSTELLATIONS IN DIFFERENT CULTURES

Different cultures see different pictures in the stars. The ancient Greeks saw the stars of Ursa Major as a bear, but those same stars were seen as a bull's leg by ancient Egyptians, as a skunk by the Sioux tribe in the American Northwest, and as a camel by North Africans!

Many different ancient and modern cultures have their own unique constellations — ones that are totally different from the **IAU's** official 88. Chinese astronomers made very careful and scientific charts of the sky long before Ptolemy did. Inuit, Australian Aboriginal, South African, Incan, Polynesian, Chumash, and Navajo are some of the cultures that have a long history of imagery and myths in the stars.

If you want to learn more about different cultures' constellations, visit these websites with the help of an adult:

* astronomy-kids.com/ancient-chinese-astronomy.html (ancient China)
* astronomy-kids.com/ancient-egyptian-astronomy.html (ancient Egypt)
* thoughtco.com/inca-star-worship-and-constellations-2136315 (Inca)
* tepapa.govt.nz/discover-collections/read-watch-play/maori/matariki-maori-new-year/whare-tapere/matariki-star-facts (New Zealand)
* legendsofamerica.com/na-astronomyculture/ (Native American)
* abc.net.au/science/articles/2009/07/27/2632463.htm (Australia)
* rmg.co.uk/discover/explore/south-african-star-myths (South Africa)

* * *

GLOSSARY: GREEK MYTHOLOGY

Centaur: A mythical creature with the head and torso of a human and the legs of a horse, who is known for wild behavior.

Cronus: One of the Titans (the son of Uranus) and ruler during the Golden Age. When Cronus was warned his children would overthrow him, he tried to eat them all!

Demigod: A person who has one human (or mortal) as a parent, and one immortal god as a parent.

Gaia: The first earth goddess in Greek mythology, and the mother of all life on Earth. She was the mother of the Titans, who were overthrown by the gods of Mount Olympus.

Gods of Mount Olympus (also known as the Olympians): The 12 gods who ruled ancient Greece from Mount Olympus during Zeus's rule: Zeus (god of the sky and the ruler of the Olympic gods), Hera (wife of Zeus and protector of heroes and women), Poseidon (god of the sea), Hades (god of the underworld), Demeter (goddess of agriculture), Athena (goddess of wisdom), Apollo (god of light and music), Artemis (goddess of the hunt), Ares (god of war), Aphrodite (goddess of beauty), Hephaestus (god of fire and the forge), Hermes (messenger of the gods).

The Golden Age: The first of the five ages of man (gold, silver, bronze, heroic, iron) and a time of great peace, prosperity, and harmony.

Immortal: A being who is capable of living forever.

Medusa: A god like creature with snakes for hair, whose face could turn anyone who looked at it to stone.

Mortal: A human who, unlike a god, cannot live forever and will die one day.

Mount Olympus: The highest mountain in Greece and the mythical home of the gods, which is why they are called Olympians.

Nereids: A group of beautiful sea goddesses (or nymphs) who protect those at sea.

Nymphs: Female goddesses of various parts of the natural world, such as the sea, the forests, or the mountains.

Oracle: A person who can hear and communicate the words of the gods to mortals, to give people advice and predict the future.

Sacrifice: In ancient Greece, a sacrifice was often an animal or food offered up on an altar, and sometimes burned, in order to gain something in return from the gods.

Satyr: A god of the natural world, who takes the form of a man with a goat's tail, legs, horns, and ears.

Titans: The children and grandchildren of Gaia and Uranus. The Titans were gods who ruled Earth during the Golden Age.

Uranus: The sky god, the father of all life on Earth, and father of the Titans.

Zeus: The youngest son of the Titan Cronus, who overthrew his father and the Titans, feeling that he and the other Olympians would do a better job as rulers.

GLOSSARY: ASTRONOMY

Asterism: An asterism is a prominent pattern or group of stars that is usually smaller than a constellation and not officially recognized by the IAU.

Astrology: The study of the belief that the stars and their positions affect the everyday lives of humans on Earth.

Astronomy: The scientific study of the stars, planets, and space.

Bayer Designation: One of the official naming systems for stars, which combines a Greek letter (like Alpha) with the Latin name of the constellation it is in, for example, Alpha Arietis. This system has made it much easier for astronomers to streamline the naming of stars, though many stars still have official proper names as well — many with Arabic or Greek origins.

Celestial: Something that relates to the sky or outer space.

Celestial sphere: An imaginary sphere in the sky around Earth that helps astronomers map the sky. Just like Earth, the celestial sphere has a northern and southern hemisphere, an equator, and north and south poles.

Circumpolar: A celestial object that moves around the north or south poles that doesn't appear to rise or set.

Ecliptic: An imaginary line in the sky along which the Sun travels. If we could see the stars in the daytime, we would see the Sun travel through one zodiac constellation to the next, making one complete round in one year.

Engineering: A profession devoted to building complicated objects, such as bridges, buildings, or complex tools that serve a practical function.

Equator: An imaginary line that runs around the middle of Earth and divides it into two hemispheres.

Equatorial constellations: Constellations that circle the sky around the celestial equator (the sky above the equator) and appear on both northern and southern sky charts.

First magnitude star: The very brightest stars in all of the sky, of which there are 22 (not including the Sun).

Hemisphere: This word means "half-sphere" in Latin, and Earth is divided along the equator into two half-spheres: the northern hemisphere and the southern hemisphere. Countries above the equator, such as the United States, Europe, China, and Russia are located in the northern hemisphere. Places below the equator are in the southern hemisphere and include countries such as Australia, New Zealand, South America, the lower parts of Africa.

IAU: The International Astronomers Union is a group of international astronomers, with a headquarters in Paris.

Their goal is to protect and promote the science of astronomy among people who study the stars and planets around the world.

Large Magellanic Cloud: A starry region that looks like a broken-off bit of the Milky Way, but is a galaxy.

Latitude: Imaginary lines that divide Earth into sections that run in the same direction as the equator and help people know their position relative to north and south.

Longitude: Imaginary lines that divide Earth into sections that run from north to south, and help people know their position relative to east and west.

Milky Way: A band of sparkling light across the sky, made up of innumerable stars. The galaxy that Earth is located within.

Navigator: A person who works out how to get somewhere, and sometimes helps to chart maps to share their knowledge with others.

North celestial pole: An imaginary point in the sky just above Earth's north pole.

Observatory: A building designed for observing the stars in a precise way.

Orbit: An orbit is a repeating curved path that one object in space takes around another, for example, when it goes around a star, a planet, or a moon. Earth orbits around the Sun.

Physics: A science that deals with the way objects and energy interact with one another. Physics in space is called astrophysics.

Polygon: A geometric shape that uses only straight lines.

South celestial pole: An imaginary point in the sky just above Earth's south pole.

Star system: A group of stars that orbit each other. A group of two stars is a binary star system. A group of three or more stars is called a multiple star system. A group with a large number of stars is called a galaxy.

Phaidon Press Inc.
65 Bleecker Street
New York, NY 10012

phaidon.com
First published 2018
Reprinted in 2018, 2019
© 2018 Phaidon Press Limited
Text and illustration copyright © Sara Gillingham

Text set in Styla Bold and Futura

ISBN 978 07148 7772 3 (US edition)
002-0419

Designed by Meagan Bennett
Edited by Maya Gartner

Printed in China